You Decide

Supercharge your Networking – Starting with LinkedIn

Relationships

Reputation

Referrals

To be is to do.
—Socrates

Networking

How do you keep in touch with somebody once you've made a connection with that person?

How are you engaging with that human being and passing information on to them?

How do you keep them informed?

How do you keep them going with technologies, with forums, with websites, with news articles?

How are you making and keeping yourself relevant?

How do you keep track of them and stay in touch with their own career evolution?

How many people who can help you, actually know you?

Copyrighted Material

You Decide: Supercharge your career and networking – Starting with LinkedIn.

Copyright© 2025 by Andrew Brümmer. All Rights Reserved.

No part of this publication may be reproduced, stored in a retrieval system, or transmitted in any form or by any means – electronic, mechanical, photocopying, recording, scanning or otherwise – without prior written permission from the publisher except for the inclusion of brief quotations in review.

It is illegal to copy this book, post it to a website, or distribute it by any other means without permission.

For information about this title or to order other books and/or electronic media, please contact the publisher.

eMail: editor@YouDecide.us

Publisher: Self Published

ISBNs:

Softcover:	ISBN- 979-8-9922772-0-3
E-book:	ISBN- 979-8-9922772-1-0

Copywrite Recognition

This book references several tools and platforms that are registered trademarks of their respective companies. LinkedIn and LinkedIn Sales Navigator are trademarks of LinkedIn Corporation, and their distinctive user interfaces and features are proprietary to LinkedIn. Calendly is a registered trademark of Calendly, LLC, known for its intuitive scheduling interface. GetDex is a product of Dex Labs, Inc., with its user-friendly design supporting contact management. Dripify, a registered trademark of Dripify LLC, is renowned for its automation and lead-generation capabilities on LinkedIn. All trademarks and interfaces mentioned herein are the property of their respective owners, and their inclusion in this book is for informational purposes only, without any implied endorsement.

To Vanessa, for the space, sanity, calmness, and keeping the house going.

Foreword

When I first met Andrew through a networking group called "Fractionals United," I assumed it would be just another casual connection. After all, I'd attended countless networking events, from happy hours to industry conferences, and thought I'd seen it all. What I didn't expect was that this meeting would transform the way I approach networking—and save me hundreds of hours in the process.

Andrew introduced me to a concept that felt almost too good to be true: automated networking. As a technical leader with over 20 years of experience in product and tech leadership, I've always prioritized building relationships. I've spent thousands of dollars on events and met some incredible people along the way. But deep down, I knew there had to be a smarter, more efficient way to expand my network—one that leveraged AI and automation.

Andrew's program was the answer I didn't know I needed. It showed me how to automate the time-consuming parts of networking, like identifying leads and initiating outreach, while leaving me free to focus on what I love most: having meaningful conversations with fascinating professionals.

What stood out most about this approach was its authenticity. This wasn't about cold sales pitches or spammy messages. Every connection I made felt genuine, targeted, and purposeful. The goal wasn't to sell—it was to build a network of professionals who, down the line, could support each other in meaningful ways.

Here's how I implemented Andrew's program:

1. **Defined My Audience:** I created customized LinkedIn queries to identify professionals I wanted to connect with. These lists ranged from 86 to 2,474 leads, tailored to specific industries, roles, or organizations.

2. **Crafted Personalized Outreach Messages:** I developed tailored messages for each cohort, ensuring they were authentic and engaging.

3. **Set Up Dripify Campaigns:** Using Dripify, I automated the outreach process, adjusting flows based on circumstances and engagement levels.

4. **Prepared for Conversations:** I created a set of go-to questions for calls to ensure conversations felt natural and flowed smoothly, whether the other party was introverted, extroverted, or somewhere in between.

5. **Let Automation Work Its Magic:** Once the campaigns were set, I let them run. Interested connections could book time directly on my calendar, and I showed up ready to engage.

The results? Over a three-month period, my LinkedIn network grew by 759 connections—most of them initiated through Dripify. Even more impressive, I booked three dozen networking calls (while working full-time) with an incredibly high success rate, including only one no-show and a few reschedules. These weren't just calls—they were opportunities to forge relationships that could one day lead to transformative partnerships, collaborations, or simply valuable exchanges of ideas.

The best part? This process stripped away the part of networking I found draining—the tedious setup—and let me focus on the rewarding part: connecting with people.

So, if you've ever felt overwhelmed by the sheer time and effort it takes to network effectively, I encourage you to give this method a try. With Andrew's guidance, I discovered that automation isn't just about saving time—it's about making room for more impactful conversations and opportunities.

Your next step: Take a moment to think about what your ideal network looks like. Who are the professionals you want to connect with? What kinds of conversations do you want to have? Then, explore tools like LinkedIn, Dripify, and Calendly to start automating the parts of networking that slow you down.

Networking doesn't have to be a grind—it can be efficient, intentional, and even enjoyable. Thanks to Andrew's program, I've redefined how I build relationships, and I'm excited for what's next. I hope you'll take the leap and discover how this approach can transform your career, too.

Mara Jorgensen

Author's Words

This book covers the journey from "Oh crap – where's the next paycheck coming from" to "This is going to be a fantastic year", along with some lessons I wish I had learned earlier in life.

This book started in March 2024 when I learned from my CEO of the risk that, without the needed funding, the company would be forced to wind down. This early awareness allowed time for a soft landing: I had time to embrace what I had learned over the following months. I cannot emphasize enough why you, like the average Andrew should-have, need to get ahead of this now. Do not wait. My life would have been in a very different spot if I had started this journey three, five, ten years ago.

I was a 53-year-old first-generation immigrant to the USA; a Chief of Staff / Chief Operating Officer with no university degree. I am at best an operational generalist; my product is people. My superpower - finding efficiency and effectiveness in nearly everything and everyone.

My professional career[1] has taken a wild, unplanned, un-organized, chaotic, exciting ride which I don't recommend for anyone. If you are of any working age, get your five or ten-year plan together. It does not matter if you change it, just have a plan!

---

[1] https://www.linkedin.com/in/andrewbrummer/

Like most professionals, I've had a lot of fun. I've seen a lot, done a lot, met a lot of people, and impacted a lot of lives as a servant-pleaser.

This juncture in March saw me looking in the mirror saying: "What now?" and slotted straight into fix-it mode. This book covers my journey from there.

I am an introverted extrovert. I get on very well in domains I own – like my company, a conference booth, a conference I plan and run, and the cul-de-sac where I put the 35,000 lights up over the festive season and meet untold numbers of strangers a night. No matter how hard I have tried, I struggled to walk up to someone at a conference event and say "Hi, my name is Andrew." It has been an irrational, illogical fear – I have worked hard to try and address this.

I had a LinkedIn network of about 1,260 people. Most of the people in that network were either friends, family, old clients, or team members – many from previous teams and clients I no longer managed. You guessed it, I had not exactly maintained relationships with anyone.

This book was written in November of the same year, and I expect it will have a few revisions as I continue down this journey of personal growth and experiencing the rewards of this book – watch this space. If you have purchased this book, please send me your receipt and an email address and I will ensure you get a free e-book version of it every time it is updated. I will highlight new learnings and add what I got wrong in this book.

What I cover in this book is an approach that works for me. It has helped me expand my network and meet some incredible people. It has given me confidence that I will be okay. More than this: it has helped me find my inner me again, given me a hunger to serve on a wide range, and solidified my understanding of what I am great at – Purpose!

I have coached countless people on what I am doing, and many of them have found their way by using online tools to create a unique method that works for them. Most importantly, this has given them a new lease on hope in this funky economic and hiring window.

This book covers learnings, lessons, wishes on hindsight, and recommendations for you. For those in a similar position to what I found myself in, we start with self-reflection and the decision to do something different.

Then it's onto the meat of *why* I wrote this book. No one walks up to a stranger in any setting and says "Hey – I have got something that can save you money, want to buy?"! You should view this section as a digital version of walking up to someone at a bar, a restaurant, or a conference when you leverage these tools.

Stop selling. In every way – STOP SELLING, stop pitching, stop asking, stop promoting. Start paying a real interest in people. Be human with people and they will reciprocate. Engage with interest and be deliberate, focus on paying it forward, introduce people to one another; serve. Forge a network around yourself.

I have learned that people I reach out to will probably not hire me. What this group – this "first degree of separation" – will do is introduce me to a second group of people whom I may not have reached out to, I probably don't have access to them, or they might not be active on LinkedIn. These people have introduced me to individuals separated to a third and even a fourth degree, who either are the people who are interested in engaging with me or know someone who will want to.

It is the second and third degree of separation that has led me to forums and bodies of people I had no idea existed, be they virtual, local, global, or face to face.

I started this journey doing everything I include here manually, and eventually moved to a hybrid mix of manual and automation, while expanding my toolkit and reach. The reason for this is simple numbers. Finding your potential customers is a challenge. Are they active on LinkedIn? Do they fall in your ideal customer profile (ICP)? Are they interested in your message? And if so, will they respond to you?

The digital world is a numbers game. While I am using LinkedIn as the pivot point here, I see no reason why this approach cannot be applied to X, Instagram, Threads, etc., or why this approach and numbers are any different from going to a conference or manning a booth.

If you need to cross the generational reach (i.e., ranging from young adults through to seasoned professionals) you will need to make sure you cover multiple platforms. Your end goal when using LinkedIn or similar platforms should be to create relationships, and to help those you meet.

I am chasing my Six to find my Two. If this doesn't make sense, let me explain how I use the numbers in LinkedIn, and why this is important.

To date, I've reached out to about 200 people per week. Of those 200, about 50 people will connect with me, and of those 50 connections, I meet with about 15 people per week – either through video, phone, or in person. About two of these people match with where I am in life and will likely end up referring or introducing me to someone or paying it forward in some form. I meet on average two people a month that can dramatically affect my professional world.

The Two – as I call them – often remain actively engaged with me. I am not saying the balance of those I meet don't want to help me but there are precious few people, right now, doing what I am trying to accomplish, and sharing the stage of life I find myself in, that could affect my path forward.

In a month, that's 800 touches → 200 connections → 60 meetings → *six engaged people* → *two that could impact my trajectory*. Let those numbers sink in. The 800 is irrelevant to a new deal – and your 6,000 connections are pure noise (other than a data input to the LinkedIn algorithms).

The Six and Two are critical!

You have got to hunt for these. One of the following are true: i) you hunt for them yourself manually, ii) you either have someone marketing on your behalf and pay their bills (between $700 and $6,000 a month) or iii) you leverage technology. It is my experience that the numbers remain persistent regardless of approach – someone must be canvasing large volumes to get you down to the six and the two – if not you, your tools. And later: someone you hire.

I trust this book helps you find your best version of yourself as you figure out your path forward.

"Only you put your foot on the floor out of bed in the morning. Only you get to decide what today looks like. Only you get to decide how you take on the day.

Table of Contents

Networking 3
Foreword 7
Author's Words 10
Why Read This Book? 19
    What This Method Meant for Me 19
    Who Does This Apply To? 20
You and LinkedIn 24
    LinkedIn!? 24
    Your LinkedIn 28
    Get Stuck into LinkedIn 34
    The Networking Effect 42
Your Brand 51
    Take Ownership of Your Brand 51
    Authors Brand 65
    Some Sample Pitches 68
    Volunteering 70
STOP – Glance Back at Those 82
Making LinkedIn Work for You 83
    Trying to Figure Out My Pitch Out 83
    To Automate or Not 85
    It's a Numbers Game 87
    Tools List 89
    Pure Automation Will Fail - Quickly 90
    Automation Can Land to Being Banned 91
    Take Your Campaign Beyond LinkedIn 92

- LinkedIn Automation 94
  - The LinkedIn Bar 94
  - High-Level Approach 94
  - Getting your Target Profiles 96
  - Automation Campaigns 99
  - They Want to Meet! 136
- Be Memorable! 143
- A Comprehensive Strategy 146
  - Tracking Your Relationship 146
  - Disengaged Contacts 147
  - An Adoption Roadmap 148
  - Networking – Supercharged 149
- Go do you! 150
- Curious? Wanna talk? 151
- Relevant Reads 152

Why Read This Book?

What This Method Meant for Me

The rewards of my journey have been vast. I have, most importantly, made some amazing friends, in a very small window of time. I have been introduced to eight professional networking forums of some sort, and four services companies with whom I will do some form of work.

I have discovered dozens of career and life changing websites that I continually pass on to others; I've been invited into three executive bodies in the Atlanta area; met owners of companies, CEOs, authors, angel investors, coaches – all of whom I would never have met.

I have authored two books with a third in writing. My professional network spans across the UK, USA, Australia, and Europe while my mentoring and coaching footprint now covers Georgia, Iraq, Uzbekistan, Rwanda, Nigeria, Botswana, the Dominican Republic, USA, and Canada to name a few.

I have had the privilege of meeting and working very closely with founders of startups, and had access to their network and the amazing world that exists to help these entrepreneurs succeed.

I have also found the energy to get myself physically active at stupid-o-clock in the morning, all while not being a morning person.

This journey has been incredible – I cannot wait to hear what you experience, where you go, how you expand and take ownership of your brand. Please let me know how you grow!

Who Does This Apply To?

The core of this book was written to help people who find themselves in the situation I did: In need of a helpful shove to jump off the cliff of indication and do something different. This book is about looking in the mirror and taking ownership of your life, your state, and doing something about it.

Students

If you are a student, this is about investing in your future. You should leverage the information here to get back in touch with your sports team, band members, and classmates from school and university – right now – while those connections are fresh. It does not matter that you don't know why, when, or where you may need them – just connect and maintain the relationship.

Network, meet, mingle, and connect where you intern. While at university, connect with your professors, sports coaches, cafeteria staff... Connect! This is a very small world, and you have no idea where people will surface again in ten years.

Add your progress through your career – make sure you link with people and then stay in touch with them. Some people will drop off, that's okay, even if you ping them annually. Stay in touch. You never know when you will need them.

Knowledge Workers

This includes the full spectrum from administration, teachers, professors, software developers, research engineers, sensor engineers, data scientists, graphic designers, lawyers, economists, policy analysts, business consultants, human resource managers, architects, medical researchers, doctors, physicians, nurses, the list goes on.

You should be connecting to anyone in your space, regardless of maturity, years in the profession, and depth of knowledge. In five years, that person you coached may well be the decision maker in your hire.

Executives

Connect with executives of all titles from the level of vice president and up. Connect, connect, connect. It astounds me how many executives hone in on their vertical and never network beyond it. The person who introduces you to your next hire will probably be in an executive position adjacent to your career.

Take the time to mingle and network in as many of the executive functional areas as possible, including face-to-face networking events. These connections will also be mixed in forums that you have no idea exist, and being linked to you will mean being able to invite you into these exclusive, invitational-only forums.

Trade-Craft workers

Like executives, artisans typically network and circle within the domains they service. First, connect with anyone in your profession. While they may not yield you business, they will know of and help you with market trends and movements.

Adjacent professions will create that network base who can recommend you because you will be a known entity.

Professions included here are electricians, plumbers, masons, painters, pipefitters, machinists, boiler makers, carpenters, landscapers, locksmiths, pest control technicians, butchers, tools and die makers, lineworkers, marine mechanics, etc.

And just before you debunk me on these, here are some LinkedIn counts I have access to through Sales Navigator within the USA: 27,000 locksmiths, 14,000 butchers, 16,000 tools and die makers, and 16,000 cabinetmakers.

Venture Capitalists, Angel Investors

All-y'all know how important this is. Enough said.

Small Business Owners

Do not underestimate the value this process can add to your business reaching your potential partners and customers. Regardless of your channel and source of customers, LinkedIn is a gold mine of opportunities and customers you have never met.

Someone in your organization should be trolling and developing relationships with your ideal customer. Your specific vertical is bound to have adjacent verticals that could help you through partnership and or cross-customer interactions.

If you are a small business owner and you want some ideas for cross-vertical and customer access examples for your vertical – please contact me – let's chat!

You and LinkedIn

LinkedIn!?

This section is focused on the average Joe, who like me, could be a servant-pleaser, a heads-down worker, a doer, someone who supports others. If you are like me, you probably have neglected your network, you battle to network at conferences and forums, and you usually stand in the back of the room watching the networking and social activities happen, in sheer frustration of not being able to meet people.

I have learned – often the hard way – that I should have taken ownership and taken care of my brand for the last 20 years. I should have made sure I had a sound, tested message and opinion of what I am great at doing. I should not have waited for the "oh crap" moment to introspect and find my inner "next" self.

Why LinkedIn

LinkedIn is the world's professional digital resume; it is the professional gravity point. Sci-Tech Today[2] did a great analysis article on LinkedIn and a number of other social platforms. I know these figures change nearly daily, I strongly encourage you to consider the volume of these

---

[2] https://www.sci-tech-today.com/stats/linkedin-statistics/

platforms' users, and engage. Cognism[3] did a similar article with additional metrics and insights. To whet your appetite and boggle your mind on what you thought would be normal, take a look at these statistics.

There are roughly 1 billion LinkedIn users worldwide of which about 310 million are active on LinkedIn in some way. Some 20 million people post articles on LinkedIn. The user base has a split of 56% males and 44% females. Surprisingly about half of the users are aged between 25 and 34. More than half (about 57%) of the traffic is on mobile devices – using portrait-form for videos and pictures could be to your advantage.

The USA hosts some 29% of this (roughly 230 million users) who are typically active between 10 AM and 12 PM on Tuesdays, Wednesdays, and Thursdays.

This is a great platform that, if you are not actively looking for work, will take you no more than an hour a week to stay engaged. Own your digital presence and be part of the algorithms that will drive your visibility when you are looking for work.

I had time to prepare for a soft-landing, most people get the notice to clear their desk without much warning. A scramble follows. Be smart, get ahead of the curve, decide what your brand is, and what is next for you.

---

[3] https://www.cognism.com/blog/linkedin-statistics

LinkedIn User Volumes

The number of people on LinkedIn is dramatic, yet the number of users that are actively engaged, or will respond to you is relatively low. Some interesting statistics searching for contacts using my profile through LinkedIn Sales Navigator yielded these stats:

	1st, 2nd, 3rd degree contacts	Active recently	Changed Jobs	Worked at a company I did	Using my ratios as a % of engagement
CTO	850,000	110,000	9,500	161	13
CFO	1m+	100,000	9,500	5	1
CPO	120,000	21,000	4,500	122	10
CLO	45,000	4,500	1,500	13	1
CMO	330,000	74,000	13,000	233	19
SW Dev	24m+	1m+	620,000	21,000	1680
DevOps	2m+	210,000	100,000	3,000	240
BA	8m+	750,000	300,000	6,000	480
Agile	1m+	190,000	53,000	2,000	160

LinkedIn is a numbers game. You must balance the time, contacts, and energy you insert to find people who will get to know you and potentially engage with you without vesting too much time or being too confident in the magic of your networking abilities.

Nearly everyone I spoke with on my journey experienced their unique version of this numbers game; nearly all of them were looking for business.

Results of My Campaign and Approach

The campaign I ran for four months had some surprising statistics. Take a look – the purpose is to highlight the long game ahead of you, which is why prioritizing and grouping the contacts above is so important.

- 34% of people I have asked to connect with me accepted my request.
- 76% of these connections engaged with me through messaging.
- 8% of the people who accepted my connection request had a one-on-one with me, either via a video call, a phone call or face-to-face.
- 25 people requested to be "unsubscribed".
- Of the 3,138 new connections, 438 of them are in active dialogue with me and 28 of them have the potential to impact my life.
- 29% of my original first-degree contacts have yet to enter the campaign.

This numbers approach will be the same whether you drive your campaign manually or by using technology and automation. The delta is the timeline – to achieve similar results by performing these activities manually will take at least ten times longer. What we run through in this book is leveraging a hybrid mix of manual and automated input.

By default, the number of people who will engage with you is limited; most will not be bothered. You are trying to get to the people who care to take the time to listen and help introduce you, share market insights, press you into forums you have not heard of, and introduce you to people and companies that you need to know.

Your LinkedIn

How Do You Show Up?

How do you show up on LinkedIn? How are you representing yourself? What does your digital profile, footprint and breadcrumb look like?

I want you to go to your LinkedIn profile and focus on your profile summary. Take 20 seconds and tell me what you read about yourself – make notes of what you glean. Do not open any of the "read more" sections; just the headline, the about summary, and your first work experience. 20 seconds is significant because that is about all the average reader or recruiter is going to give you. What do you note down? No sure of yourself – ask someone else to do the same on your profile and tell you what they learn about you.

Once you've done this, go through two or three of these LinkedIn profiles and do the same.

- Jon Keel: https://www.linkedin.com/in/jonkeel/
- Thomas Helfrich: https://www.linkedin.com/in/thomashelfrich/
- Ganesh Ariyur: https://www.linkedin.com/in/ganeshariyur/
- Tom Wardman: https://www.linkedin.com/in/tom-wardman/
- Alanna Mahone: https://www.linkedin.com/in/alanna-mahone/
- Tim Lesko: https://www.linkedin.com/in/timlesko/
- Tom Freiling: https://www.linkedin.com/in/tomfreiling/

Compare the level of insights you garnered in 20 seconds from your profile against the others. What is the picture you learned from their profile vs yours?

Now do the same exercise and spend two minutes on your profile, expanding the "read more" sections. Go wherever the information takes you and when you get bored, jump to the next session. Jot down as many functional things and capabilities you note about yourself that are written, posts, summaries, jobs, and recommendations. It is important you stay within the text in your profile and not what you meant or intended when you wrote; remember the reader does not have the privilege of your mind.

Let's do the same for the profiles you used earlier; spend two minutes on each. What did you learn about them and how does it contrast onto yours? Recruiters who busy themselves with your profile are going to spend a couple of seconds there, not minutes.

Your headline is crucial. So are the first 100 words in your "about" section,

On most LinkedIn profiles the "headline" represents the current job title you hold and not what you can do. Remember: The reader (or AI) is hunting and will give you the benefit of brevity as they decide to further expand on your profile and learn more. It is your job to grab their attention before they move on to the next profile.

When you talk about yourself, you must separate your profile from the thousands of profiles, which will be like yours. It's therefore important to steer away from what is natural. Be punchy, provocative, and insightful while remaining factual avoiding exaggeration.

Your Connections

Most of us gather our LinkedIn connections around people we've met as peers, clients, and friends. Looking at your LinkedIn contacts will tell you that your network has very few who can truly help you move forward or find a new job.

For the most part, your network will be in a similar place it was when you left those jobs. This is especially true if you are a career progressor, someone constantly changing up or pivoting your next steps. While some of your contacts will absolutely lean in, a lot of these people probably can't help you pivot or progress your career.

Create a list of your connections who you think are impactful, relevant, important, and could potentially help you. Make sure to note their career trajectory, title changes, and what they've done over the jobs they have held. List probing questions that will uncover what and why they have done to get to where they are.

I did a similar activity and created three separate lists of people: Those I needed to contact socially, people I've noticed are on a career trajectory that could potentially help me through their career choices, and lastly the people I respect, have held significant positions with, or who could coach and nudge me in the right direction.

My journey looked like this: I had about 1,260 connections at the start of this campaign; I guesstimated that about 5% of my LinkedIn network – about 60 people –

were able to aid me in some way. More may be interested in what I've done with my life, how I've moved on in my career, and what my horizons held. I started by looking at these 60 LinkedIn profiles and decided to reach out to them through individual programs. This step I call "profiling your network".

Your Existing Network's Value

If you are anything like me, you are probably going to find it difficult to read through and analyze the profiles in your LinkedIn network. Figuring out who is there, who you remember, where your relationships are... It's tough (and embarrassing)!

The following profile data points will help you identify the people you should get in touch with:

- When you connected with them.
- How long you have known them.
- What was your relationship with them.
- Their job title changes.
- LinkedIn activities such as posts and comments.
- When last they were active on LinkedIn.
- Their relocation and career pivot history.
- Career progression in and out of your skills vertically.

You'll learn the following as you go through your contacts:

- You have not spoken to most of them for five, ten, or more years.

- Many have not significantly changed jobs since you last worked with them.
- Most of them cannot offer any fundamental impact on your job search or future progression.
- There are a handful of people you know really well and are great people who will help without question.
- Some of them will have progressed in their careers, some may have retired, or hold positions that may be that of coach, mentor, or advisor for you.
- You may have a few contacts able to be sponsors for you in a target company, board position, job title, or forum.

You need to use your LinkedIn to meet a new elk of people; connections that will form your career pivot landing point. This means breaking away from what is comfortable and broadening the scope of the people you deal with.

What you are trying to uncover are those contacts you can message: "I have been a remiss and not spoken with you, I am reforging contacts" vs "HELP!!!" You are also identifying those contacts best left dormant for now. The key is to start a few outreaches with specific content and messages to a specific group of people.

This is important because you want people who can help you to engage, and you want to restart communications with the contacts you have not been in touch with for a while. I leverage both approaches as I triage my network.

LinkedIn and LinkedIn Sales Navigator

Leverage the search filters which start with 1st degree connections. From there, filter it down to companies, your city, active users on LinkedIn, those who've recently changed jobs, to name a few. The reason you'll want to use LinkedIn Navigator over LinkedIn Premium include:

- Massively increased search filters including "last active" on LinkedIn, last job, years in current company, and years in current position.
- Deep insights on the connection including relationship history and their LinkedIn timeline.
- Account / Company details and alerts including your access to it, and the ability to build your relationship map into the company, posting, and hiring insights.
- Lead list recommendations including people you are tracking, executive movements at accounts you are following, and recommended leads based on your LinkedIn interactions
- Ability to discover potential connections at an account and insights to build relationships through the relationship explorer and the development of relationship maps for each account.
- Connect Sales Navigator with your CRM (customer relationship management) to keep data up-to-date and streamline your workflow.
- See when and how a buyer has expressed interest in your company or services.

Exporting your Contacts

All of these tools you will experience, and use are great at doing what they were designed to do. None of them will offer you the ability to sort, mine, manipulate, extract specific profiles. Step in Excel and Google sheets.

If you are familiar with Excel or Google Sheets, exporting your contacts will help you mine, filter and bundle LinkedIn URLs for follow-up (manually or automated). This export ability includes limited data such as email address, company, position, and connection date.

Using automation tools you are able to export additional data, including email address and phone number (where available), the contact's title, company, city, and country. Using data merge techniques in a spreadsheet you will be able to combine the data records to help narrow down your target lists.

As a side note: It is always good to do cyclical exports of your contacts. This is especially important to protect you in the event you do something silly and get yourself banned.

Get Stuck into LinkedIn

If Time is Your Enemy

If time is not on your side and you need to get leads and networking going, I recommend you pause here and start looking at your LinkedIn contacts. Get in touch with the people who match the criteria you've set to help your networking campaigns.

No, I do not mean "help you in a sticky situation" or "find a job", I mean people who can help you extend your network. Engage with them and start building your second and third-degree contacts. Your existing contacts are a great opportunity to expand your network to people, forums, and bodies that can further your career.

I cannot emphasize how important it is to not "sell" yourself, no matter your desperation – your desperate pleases will fall on deaf ears of people you have not maintained relationships with, often even with people you have maintained relationships with.

That means... don't ask for a job, an opportunity, work, "Can you help me?", or "Do you know someone who can help me?" By doing this, you are broadcasting desperation and showing disrespect to your contact, especially if you have not maintained an informed relationship with them. It's more than likely you will get a response along the lines of "Good to hear from you! We should talk sometime!" – and then... The sound of crickets!

I do recommend that you explain your situation, state the problem, tell them what you are doing, how you are moving forward, and that you are expanding your network. Apologize for not being in touch (regardless of them not contacting you) and tell them you would love to catch up sometime. Demonstrate ownership and action.

Re-engage with People You Know

Your goal is to get people to talk with you. Don't expect any more than about 20% of your existing connections to respond to you. Take the time to lean in, engage with contacts and share what you are doing.

Start developing a communication platform with these connections so that you are engaged with them on a recurring basis in a way that they experience you versus you just doing a massive outreach. You need to figure out how you echo yourself through LinkedIn messaging within the tenor and tone that that person knows you.

Keep and safeguard the list you created above. Clearly mark each contact as a priority, or normal. Make sure this list includes LinkedIn URLs (this will be important later). Now, start re-developing relationships with them.

Don't scrub Your Contacts – Not Yet

While counterintuitive, you should delay cleaning out your contacts for the day when you have a truly great network, a great job, a lot of money in the bank, and no need for digital reach. LinkedIn algorithms need to know you are relevant, liked, and popular as you start ramping up your online activities. It is also important for rankings.

I made this fatal mistake throughout my career. As I changed jobs, I cleaned out my network by removing people for a variety of reasons:

- I believed I would not engage with them again in the foreseeable future.
- Separation of church and state – walking away from the past.
- Significant swivel and moving on with my career.

- I thought of them as people for whom I no longer held regard or appreciation – whatever the reason.

This was not smart. I dented my connection numbers (which we will cover later), I lost a link to some people who decided to pivot or accelerate their careers, and I dropped my connection and follower volumes. Most importantly, it seriously dented my ability to reach new second and third-degree contact stretch and outreach.

Many of these people may have been in different, higher, pivoted positions, in different organizations, chasing different verticals. By removing them from my network, I effectively removed all of their second and third-degree connections from my reach – why this matter is covered later.

Long-Lost Connections

The first thing you can do is to send a simple message to the people you've not engaged with for some time: "Hey, I'm making a pivot change. I'll keep you updated as life progresses. We haven't spoken for a while, and I have been remiss. Would love to chat with you and catch up." Be honest, take ownership, and start communicating.

The key here is to find the handful of people in your network who know you and have progressed their careers. They can help you with words of wisdom, offer insights and counsel, and will love to help you find your feet.

Do everything you can to meet these people face to face. As you learn, keep them updated on the progress of your journey and share both failures and successes. Don't leave them behind – and most important of all – keep the relationship alive. It will be nearly impossible to resurrect these if you let them slip into nothingness again.

It is infinitely easier to leverage people who know you for some quick words of wisdom to help you accelerate your campaign.

Get Started

Now that you have a *sense* of a sense of what your profile is, this question remains: Is it good enough to draw people in? Will your profile "sell" you? When you hit send on those first messages to your existing contacts, how are they going to read you, who do they see, and what do they take away? If it's not up to scratch, they will pop in, take a peek at your profile, then head off to the next task.

Some of us are in privileged positions where our network – our online connections or friends in real life – are in places that can immediately affect our careers. They have the power to immediately get us referenced, even hired. Sadly, these contacts are in the minority, and most people are where I found myself before I started this journey.

My recommendation is that you get in front of it – now! Get your foot out of your cozy career bed and take ownership of your choices while you are not looking for work from a position of desperation. Leverage your youth and time to your advantage to create a formative, deep, impactful network, so that when you do get there, you have the network to fall back on. Decide – and do. Don't wait for the job, company, or career mishap to happen. Small increments of recurring activities now will place you in a healthy position to glide straight onto your next opportunity later.

Getting into these good habits without unnecessary pressure will serve you well, especially while you are in a comfortable job and your energy and mindset are in line. Start rebuilding relationships now, refresh, rekindle – get moving!

> *You're the only one who gets to decide what today looks like, how people experience you, whom you get in contact with, and whom you start solidifying as a pivot move in the future.*

Regardless of your age, there is an exciting journey ahead of you. You will learn things about yourself that were never obvious. You will create an energy about yourself and set the stage for a great pivot. I experienced immense value through this journey. What will you take from this?

Do or do not, there is not try!

Sample Outreach Messages

Close Influential Contacts

Here is an example note I sent to people I knew could help point me in the right direction. The results included video calls, coffee, and meals where some points of my approach were challenged, solidified, validated, and changed.

"I trust this finds you well.

It has been a while since we last spoke or worked together. Would love to catch up. I have some changes on the go and wanted to fill you in, find out what you are up to, and ask for your assistance where you are able. I see you are now retired and am hoping I could leverage some of your brain trust.

You will remember that I am full of energy, a go-getter, a driver, and always looking for answers. Frustratingly the part of my world I have always battled with is asking for help and self-promotion – which is what I must do now. In these vulnerable states, I am wondering if I could ask you for some of your words and guidance.

A brief backdrop on what I am doing now: I'm on a career pivot right into fractional COO / Chief of Staff for startups (up to 500 people) in the tech, software, and professional service space. I am doing pro-bono coaching and mentoring and working with single-person startups to help them find their feet.

My focus remains on the creation of powerful leadership teams and the relentless drive toward efficiencies (time and money).

Thanking you in advance for any pointers and words."

General Network Outreach

For other contacts – those who were not in a position to assist me with career changes and where a possible impact on my job hunt seemed slim – I sent the following message:

"If you have not heard I am venturing back into the consulting world (as a Fractional Executive) where I am merging my consulting and executive experiences ("Fractional" being part-time executive). I continue to be involved in LifeQ and driving the vision.

My focus in the fractional world is helping fractured leadership teams (executives all the way down) as well as driving efficient use of resources (people, time, and money). In this fractional space I am currently mixing with hundreds of executives, some amazing people across the exec suite – talk about fire-hose learnings!

Would love to catch up – I have been remiss as I have been heads down keeping my world spinning."

Getting back in touch with your network will feel odd, and sometimes embarrassing. Face it, accept it, deal with it, and start moving forward.

Start now!

The Networking Effect

You will encounter many doors in your professional journey. I encourage you to open every door and peek inside; you never know what you will find (or miss if you don't).

It is important to keep in mind that your networking is NOT just about LinkedIn, that will fail. Your networking journey must include at least industry networking events where you get to meet people face to face. You should find ways to pay-it-forward; be this writing, blogging, coaching, volunteering, giving... anything. It is an important foundation for your professional presence.

You need to own your networking, be purposeful and deliberate. It will not happen by accident or through the normal course of the day. You have to drive every interaction, outreach, and event attendance.

My Networking Journey

My networking journey – and most of my story – centers around the executive space. We all have our history paving the way to where we are today, and your version of this part of the journey, regardless of your position, is meaningful. Take note of the expansive growth I saw when I began exploring what is all out there – I simply had to make what I found relevant.

The diagram below shows my networking journey. Both people and LinkedIn were pivotal to the expansion of this network. Each of the human figures represents someone that I met through networking, and they were either directly able to change my life or introduce me to life-changing forums or people.

This is the Network Effect – without selling

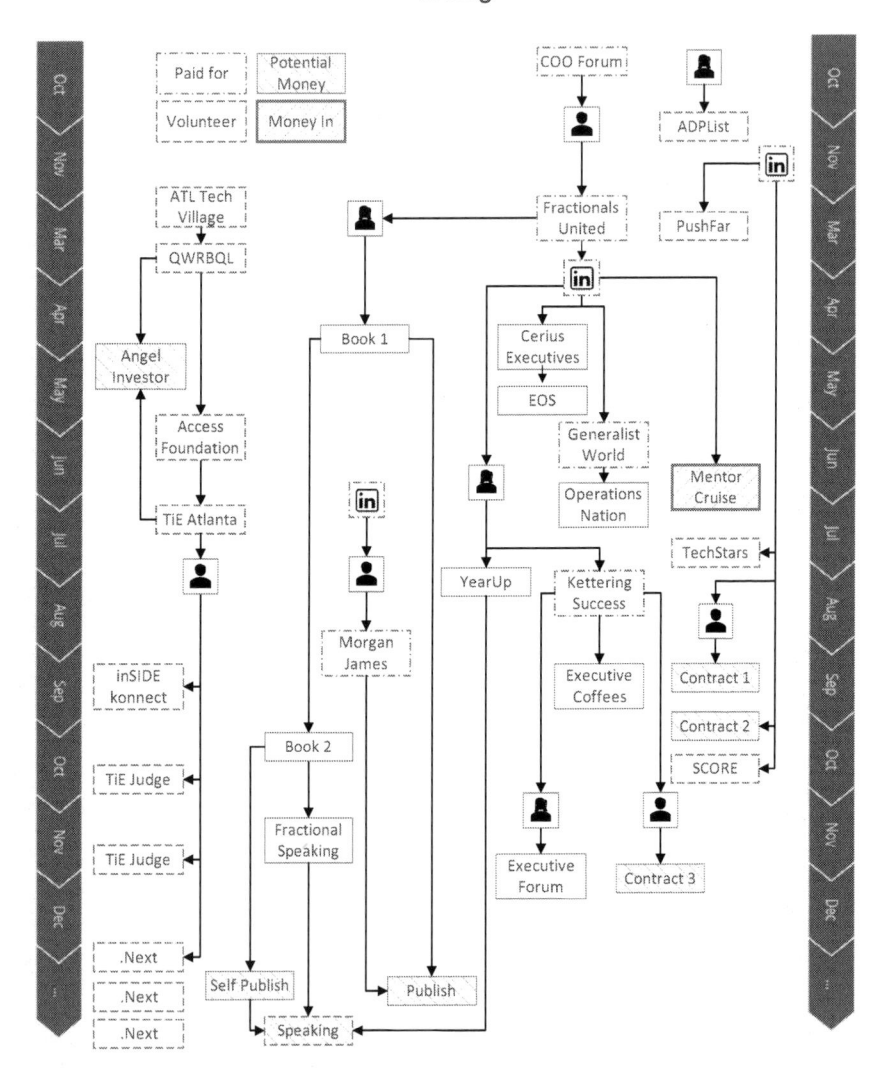

My journey started with the COOForum[4]; a global body of Chief Operating Officers providing a peer-based professional development community exclusively for high-performing operations executives, offering monthly meetings, workshops, and an online platform to connect and share insights. This is a paid-for forum. Someone there (thank you, Josh!) pointed me to Fractionals United[5] (FrUn).

FrUn is a global body (mainly featuring users from the US) of executives that make themselves available to companies as a part-time executive – imagine long-term consultants with organizational accountability – meaning you fill a function and run it until you need to hire someone to replace yourself. FrUn has interest groups like Operations, Marketing, Sales, State-specific, etc. Joining this community requires a small fee.

I chose to attend any and all of these events to cross-network and meet people. It was here I realized I needed a digital profile campaign focused on LinkedIn.

I met Kimberly at one of these networking events. She pressed me into LinkedIn posting and suggested I share my knowledge by writing books. To date I have written *Leading Magnanimously*, *Hope is a Powerful Emotion*, and this one. Four more are in the works.

---

[4] https://www.cooforum.net/
[5] https://www.fractionalsunited.com/

In another of these groups, I was introduced to Generalist World[6] – a platform for people who have many skills in many verticals. Being a generalist makes it incredibly hard to synthesize value propositions and focus hiring activities. It is a community platform designed to support individuals with non-linear, interdisciplinary careers by helping them navigate and thrive in diverse professional paths. They offer resources, courses, networking opportunities, and learnings tailored for adaptable professionals who excel across multiple domains. This group is fantastic, and Milly, Generalist World's founder, is an incredible person who has rallied an amazing group of people who pay it forward in unspeakable ways.

Generalist World got me exposed to Operations Nation[7], a community-powered knowledge hub for operations leaders, offering resources and events to support professional growth. With over 1,500 members, including COOs, VPs, and Heads of Operations from startups and scaleups, this platform facilitates learning and networking among peers.

Through FrUn I was introduction to Cerius Executives[8]– providers of interim, fractional, and direct-hire executive leadership across all management disciplines. They offer customized solutions tailored to a business' needs. Their network comprises thousands of vetted

---

[6] https://www.generalist.world/
[7] https://operationsnation.com/
[8] https://ceriusexecutives.com/

executives ready to address challenges such as company scalability, sales growth, cultural changes, and leadership gaps.

Cerius Executives led me to Entrepreneurial Operating System (EOS), a business framework comprising simple concepts and practical tools designed to help entrepreneurs and leadership teams clarify, simplify, and achieve their vision. By focusing on six key components – Vision, People, Data, Issues, Process, and Traction – EOS aims to instill focus, discipline, and accountability throughout an organization, fostering a cohesive and functional leadership team.

MentorCruise[9], another online platform I accessed via FrUn, connects individuals seeking mentorship with industry experts across fields such as leadership, accountability coaches, software engineering, product management, AI, design, operations, and business. It offers personalized, one-on-one guidance to help mentees learn new skills, launch projects, and advance their careers. MentorCruise is a paid-for mentoring website where I have, to date, met three people I mentor. Two are based in the US (in Georgia and California) and one lives in Australia.

FrUn's small groups lead me to Kettering Success[10]. This is an invitation-only, curated, executive networking organization based in Atlanta, and comprises of 1,300+ senior-level executives across various industries. Members

---

[9] https://mentorcruise.com/
[10] https://ketteringsuccess.org/

adhere to a "pay it forward" principle, actively assisting each other with business ideas, opportunities, mentorship, and introductions.

I met Paul, the founder and CEO of a company called QWRBQL, at the Atlanta Tech Village. Paul and I worked to prepare a funding pitch, which led to an introduction to the Access Foundation, a non-profit focused on minority startups through the Atlanta chapter of TiE Global. The Access Foundation team invited me to be part of a number of their programs including LIFT (where I learned of inSIDEkonnect, the fastest-growing e-procurement platform), PCIC (as a judge), and Hackathon 2024 (as a judge). I look forward to involvement with many more to come.

The long and the short? These bodies have put me in touch with people across the world I would, on an average day, never have found or met. Of the countless people I've met, many might not remember me. However, the opposite is true: Some of these connections led to valuable relationships where we know one another well and regularly stay in touch. In each of these forums, you'll get out what you put in.

By volunteering self-learning, and mixing with peers on these forums, I have had ample opportunities to pitch, but also to hear myself pitch. I got to observe others, and I received critical guidance on how to improve. I even learned about things I waffle on...

I recognize that it is improbable for someone in these forums to hire me, however, they know someone, who knows someone who will hire me. I have met numerous people – often separated to the fourth degree – who have initiated hiring discussions, which as of writing this, I have kept at abeyance in favor of the company I am working for right now.

A key takeaway of my journey is this: The healthy balance of forum networking, in-person events, volunteering, and LinkedIn helped to place me in a position of relative comfort. I have some money coming in (what a great sense of comfort!), and while being a 50+-year-old generalist executive, I know there is a wonderful journey ahead of me yet.

I cannot emphasize the dramatic effect volunteering has had for, to, and within me. It was positively pivotal to finding my way and opened many doors.

Volunteering has helped demonstrate that I am not just about me. The forums have opened my eyes to a wider, more sound way of thinking in my profession, and I have stepped out of my comfort zone to experience a non-political environment where I could listen to executive peers and truly hear how they think and execute. Startup forms were where I met numerous of my target customers in a non-threatening manner and learned two things: what they honestly need and how I can add value. LinkedIn has given me a platform to find like-minded people whom I respect and would never have met. It has also given me a platform to find my next clients.

Why Do All This, You Ask?

I know... You want to know why I do all of this. Simple: I love people, and I love engaging with people to see them thrive and win. My brain moves fast and having all of these moving targets keeps me stimulated. I chose to own tomorrow and make it happen.

My five-year life goal is to take an RV and travel through the USA. My ten-year goal is to do the same through Europe, Australia, and New Zealand. Then cruise around the world. There isn't much time to get to a place where I can do all of these... And while I am doing this, I have a deep desire to pass my world of experience onward.

"Get busy living or get busy dying."

- Shawshank Redemption

Your Brand

Take Ownership of Your Brand

To Write or Not

I started blogging in April as a result of a Fractionals United dinner. After we met, Kim said "Andrew, you have some stories here, you need to write. Blogs, short-form text, long-form book. Just write!" My response was a resounding "no". Writing won't work. I don't have the patience. No way I can write, I told her. Kim encouraged me to take thirty minutes a day: get out of bed half an hour earlier and start blogging about leadership, "because it is clearly close to your heart".

I did. Thirty minutes of morning blogging turned into hours of content creation, which turned into the start of *Leading Magnanimously*, my first book on leadership. *Leading Magnanimously* took me four months to write. I learned the importance of well-structured thoughts and the book's format massively helped me plan and write book two and three. Two non-fictions later, I am busy with my first fiction and have ideas for more.

Like my experience with writing, I fully expect you will surprise yourself! Get started and figure out your version of yourself. Writing is a great way to claim – but also gain – insights, knowledge, and credibility in the space your skills occupy.

If you don't know where to start, don't worry. There are great guides and lots of guidance on writing. I learned that getting up slightly earlier and having a fixed structure for your book in place – like a detailed table of contents – worked amazingly well. This allowed me to carry this "plan" with me and whenever I had a quiet time, I recorded myself speaking about the topics. Mornings offered time to convert the audio into text and to make sense of the ramblings.

Wondering what is keeping you from doing this? There is a myriad of reasons why blogging, trolling your network, reaching out, and writing will not work for you. To combat this, read the book *No Excuses*[11]. In short, it will guide you towards the mirror and provide practical strategies on how you can take control of your life and eliminate those excuses that result in inaction or non-favorable actions. I cannot recommend this book strongly enough.

Another book to read is *Know What You're For*[12]. It is a fantastic book for anyone looking to transform their approach to work and life. It'll be a great follow-up to *No Excuses*.

Decide! Do!

Just in case I am not being clear: Start creating. Write blogs, and make regular, provocative posts or simple videos. Start creating your public credibility footprint. It is not

---

[11] No Excuses by Brian Tracey
[12] Know What You're For: A Growth Strategy for Work, an Even Better Strategy for Life by Jeff Henderson

important to do it weekly, just do it on a cadence that matches the rhythm of your creation – and make sure what you are posting is great content. Do not put frivolous stuff up – and if you have – take it down.

I cannot implore you enough to decide to do something proactive. Start by waking up thirty minutes earlier tomorrow morning and make time for your LinkedIn profile. Get started with the steps above. Spending this time on yourself is as important as looking after your physical wellbeing.

How do You Show Up?

Take screenshots of how you show up today. Go to your LinkedIn profile, search for yourself on Goole, Bing, Duck-Duck-Go, etc. What are the first things the world sees about you? How far down the list are you? How do you show up digitally?

Beyond LinkedIn and the digital world, how do you appear? There is no wrong answer, just a question. In meetings, on Zoom sessions, for coffee, lunch, for the team event? How do you dress? What do you wear? What are your friends and family seeing? What are you trying to portray? Are you animated? Are you quiet in meetings? Do you come across as pushy? Are you the energy in the room?

Put a few reminders in your calendar to take a selfie or screenshot of yourself in meetings, during the day, and/or late afternoon. Don't analyze them until your capture window is complete. At the end of this, look through the pictures – what do you see? What do your clothing and color palettes say about you? What is the meaning behind your energy, your smile, the frown, or the focused look? What do you see and where is the delta between what you're seeing and what you're aspiring to be? Ask those close to you to jot down brief notes about how they experienced you and send them to you after your capture window.

Try to look past your perception of how you present yourself. See yourself through the eyes of the people experiencing you. You can do this by asking your friends, current and especially past colleagues, your direct reports, and your peers – the ones that are closest to you at work – to share their experiences of you.

Ask them what they see. Ask them to have a look at your profile and to highlight the deltas between what your profile says you do, have done, and can do. Let them give you an outside-in view of what you're about and how you're presenting yourself.

When you Google yourself, what does the search say? Where do you rank on the search platform? I fully expect you could not care less now. However, imagine you have just lost your job, right now, and you need to start looking for something else. What is your footprint when people look for you?

How are you presenting yourself on LinkedIn, and how closely does this match your resume? Taking small regular steps in getting your profile ready, trickle-feeding the engine, and expanding your network today is a heck of a lot easier than scrambling when you desperately need the work.

LinkedIn Profile Basics

Everything in your profile should serve a purpose: Images, links, text, titles. Everything must be placed purposefully. There should be no fluff, no platitudes, no gravy messages, no filler text. Remember the profiles I shared earlier in this book? Have another peek – you'll find the links on page 22.

Your Banner

Your banner – the space at the top of your profile – should be SCDS: Simple, clean, and damn sexy. It should convey what you are a part of and what you do in attractive, attention-grabbing graphics.

Profile Picture

The profile picture is down to the vertical you find yourself in, the job title, or the people you will be working with. By default, most profiles are presented as business casual. The most important part is your posture. Smile with your eyes, your posture, and your mouth.

Your Headline

Make your headline scream what you do. Here are some examples:

- CHRO | CPO | Executive Vice President, Human Resources | Chief Culture Carrier | Learning and Talent Management ➤ Connecting People and Vision
- CEO | COO | President | Owner | Entrepreneur | Strategy | Manufacturing | Building Materials | Operations Excellence

- Chairman & CEO | 3X Founder | Book Publisher | Premium Ghostwriter | Forbes Business Council | Inc. 5000
- VP Elevating Business Performance, Growth & Efficiency Through Digital Transformation & IT Innovation | Enterprise Business Systems & Architecture | ERP Excellence | P&L Management | Data, AI, RPA | Process Optimization
- COO | CoS | Create Autonomous Teams | Advisor | Solutionist | Save Time & $$ while Maximizing Sales | Leadership Coach | Guiding Tech & Professional Services to Scalable Growth
- Founder Assessor | CxO | Startup Enabler | Advisor | Solutionist | Multiplier | CEO Whisperer | Power Facilitator

Your Posts

LinkedIn's ranking engine takes the full balance of your profile participation into account. To demonstrate a healthy active account it is important to participate on LinkedIn. You should do all of the following:

- Simply react to other people's posts. Like them, celebrate them, etc.
- Comment on other user's posts with comments that create a reaction and/or engagement with other people.
- Repost other user's posts with comments to create reactions and/or engagements on your profile.

- And lastly, create and share posts, images, and/or videos of your own. This allows for – you've guessed it – reaction and/or engagement, which the ranking engine loves.

About you

The first 50 words should describe you in a nutshell. Here are some examples; notice how few filler words are used.

- A leader who combines strategic insight with operational excellence, I create environments where HR initiatives support business success and drive employee satisfaction. With over 20 years of progressive experience across various industry sectors, my proactive approach to using technology and data has transitioned HR teams into vital business partners.
- I am outstanding at founder assessments and helping inspire founders and teams. I extend CEOs to multiply themselves and reclaim their calendars. I am a sound business, product, and operations soundboard–safe logic-bomb multiplier. I'm a get-the-job-done, hands-on exec with the insights, wisdom, knowledge, energy, passion, and capability to help startups scale.
- Innovative Manager and Change Agent with proven success in building centers of excellence and sustained performance in start-up, turnaround, and rapid expansion environments in sales, operations, and manufacturing. Strategic business acumen is consistently demonstrated in

- the development of initiatives that generate increased gross profitability, optimal productivity, and customer satisfaction.
- Publishing industry C-suite veteran, entrepreneur, and pioneer in digital publishing, founder and CEO of NASDAQ digital publisher. I've represented, collaborated with, and published multiple NY Times best-selling authors, professional athletes, celebrity musicians, journalists, political influencers, and notable thought leaders.

When you write this, run it through AI like ChatGPT, CoPilot, or something similar with specific prompts to make it punchy, short, informative, and to the point. Remember: The first 50 words are all that is visible without expanding and reading more.

Job Titles and Descriptions

You could include a two-line summary of your employer in the description. I have not experienced a marked difference in learning about the person with or without this. My preference is to allow the person to click through the company icon if they want to know more about the company you work for. Rather use your "screen time" to promote yourself.

Your goal is to power-punch information in absolute brevity while being provocative and relevant. Your profile should be a resounding statement of what you have achieved. Some examples include:

- Led a cross-functional team of 10, launched a new product with a 25% revenue increase.

- Implemented a digital marketing strategy boosting web traffic by 40% and social media engagement up by 50%.
- Refreshed project management tools, reduced project turnaround by 30%.
- Achieved and retained a 98% customer satisfaction rate.
- Secured $1 million in VC funding to support operational expansion.
- Cost-saving initiative reducing annual expenses by $500,000.
- Received 'Employee of the Year' recognizing growth and culture.
- Authored and published a research paper garnering 1,000+ citations.

Do not waffle; do remove filler words. Every word you have in your profile matters and should be there intentionally. Your profile is meant to be a powerful summary of what you have been capable of doing with the intent to brag about what you could do if someone were to hire you. Talk about your capabilities by bragging about your successes.

Yes – I said that – BRAG! Being humble about your successes is not what you should be presenting here. Having spoken with hundreds of people in the last months, I am consciously aware that bragging about ourselves is one of the hardest – almost anti-social – things to do. Most people detest this and steer away from it. You should find a way to see this form of bragging as something positive. You are sharing your success and there is nothing wrong with doing it proudly.

Leverage LinkedIn for what it is: your personal advertising and credibility banner. It should be able to speak for you when you are not in the room. When you are networking, you can speak about all the stories, the context, and the color of how you got to where you are.

Character Presentation

You can also use your LinkedIn profile to present your character. Show a little of who you are as a human because you are not just work. However, be concise. Share your causes, hobbies, passions in life... No, it is not Facebook or Instagram. It's definitely not TikTok. Don't go there. Use LinkedIn to give a subtle hint about your interest in life. I'll share my list. What do you learn about me from this small block of text?

- 35,000+ Christmas lights playing to 200+ songs
- Build rustic live-wood-work furniture
- Climbed Kilimanjaro
- Bred and sold saltwater creatures
- Ballroom dancing
- Youth group, missions, church leadership
- Off-Road Rescue Volunteer
- Relocated from SA to USA to UK to USA

Be sure to include your volunteering and pro-bono work. This is part of your value creation and credibility. The message of how you are impacting the world around you is important. Make it count, for you, and those who could learn from you. I share more on this topic later.

LinkedIn is THE Professional Gravity Point

Once you have your "about me" summary, job description, and some points of interest written well, you will be able to repurpose it across other professional networking platforms. These include Glassdoor, The Ladder, and GoFractional, to name a few.

Keep in mind that every recruiter, every background check, and every "who are you" search inevitably lead back to LinkedIn – all of them. Make yours count.

Only you get to decide if you are the bus driver of your career, or a passenger on that same bus with someone else driving.

(Neither is wrong – just own your decision)

Make Yourself Memorable

In every interaction, without being obtuse, overbearing, too braggy, boastful or noisy – you must make yourself memorable. Right now, doing what you do, in the areas of your immediate impact, there are tens of thousands of people changing jobs, pivoting, and networking. You need to find a way to make yourself stand out.

Everyone says: "I am special" and "I have what you need" or "Come buy from me" and "Trust me, I've been there; done that".

What was the last networking event or meeting you attended? How much do you remember about that person and (if you can remember it) why do you remember it? What stood out for you?

How do you reposition yourself so that you are remembered? You are going to meet two to five hundred people in the next eight months. How are you going to stand out? How do you position yourself as the one in twenty that I will absolutely remember and want to engage with?

It's worth remembering that people gravitate to those they like. People tend to engage with, go drinking, and do business with people they remember, especially if they remember you fondly. In the image presented in the previous section (see page 36) there are seven people who took the time to get to know me and have already changed my life. They were all relevant and memorable.

People are not going to remember the fact that you work hard; there are hundreds of thousands of people who "work hard" within your profession. They're not going to remember you are a software developer, a lawyer, or an executive in Atlanta; there are two thousand COOs in Atlanta – I am one person.

To compound this challenge, there is also a crowd of people masquerading in your space as skilled team members, with many of them being brand new to the space. You need to separate yourself from this noise – it is easiest to do this ahead of the interactions than trying to unplug yourself from the blasting stereo you have been cast into.

Here are some examples to make yourself memorable:

- Be fully engaged and present, full of energy when you meet with people, have that extra cup of coffee, and make sure your sessions are at or within your peak energy window.
- Have a clear and concise message – think elevator pitch – about who you are and the value you provide.
- Avoid using your job title when you introduce yourself – rather focus on what you do. Referring to your job title immediately casts you into the preconceived box that person has for that title.
- Share a personal story about your journey or situation in life. This can be about the job you are trying to hold onto, hobbies you have, your children's successes, or lives you have impacted. Be vulnerable – it's what makes us human.
- Always offer value first, always reach out first, and always pay-it-forward first. This can be through forums, URLs, introductions, books, contacts, and time.
- Be a connector – connect, connect, connect. You may not know how to help someone. Someone you know, however, can help. Introduce them to one another after checking with both parties if you may do this.
- Engage with your audience via their platform of choice. This means if they prefer WhatsApp, Telegram, another social media platform – it does not matter – engage with them there. Email,

LinkedIn, phone calls, coffee... Be present on the platform your audience prefers to be engaged with.
- Thoughtfully follow-up. Be mindful of the information you share with them, their state of career, and networking. Share thoughtfully in spaces you believe will impact them, whether it is as introductions, books, conferences, reports, tidbits, etc.

Your goal is to leave that person with an impressionable memory of you that you are worth keeping close at hand. Either as someone always on their mind, or instantly recognizable when you re-engage with them.

Authors Brand

Some of My Stories

When I'm on a video call, you'll see a rich background filled with flags, concert tickets, references to Minions, Star Wars, Cards Against Humanity, items from startups I have been involved with, celebratory bottles of wine, bubbly, and whiskey, and collectibles from Africa, England, and Canada.

If asked about my hobbies, I open up about saltwater breeding (let's talk 'bout RBTA, Phytoplankton, Tigger-Pods, Sparky's Reef Farm), holiday lights displays (35,000 Christmas lights programmed to more than 200 songs for my annual Ardunan Lights), live-edge woodworking (I've constructed bedroom sets, mirror jewelry boxes, Hi-Fi stands, cabinets, armoires, bathroom vanities), my writing, and the one-on-one coaching I do voluntarily.

I treat every phone call or video meeting as the first one – every time. I've decided to be fully and completely present in the discussions. I am a natural introvert, yet I switch to extrovert in the company of people I know or when I'm in a safe space. I enjoy people, learning, sharing, and growing.

I work to make sure every discussion is memorable. When I'm coaching, or meeting people, or making introductions, or simply helping people find one another... Everything is geared towards helping individuals move forward.

I completely lean in to help by sharing what I've learned. I always challenge myself by asking how I am helping other people evolve themselves as their careers move forward. How am I helping them find their feet and be larger than life? How am I aiding them to form part of their brand and make decisions tomorrow?"

People walk away from a call with me feeling heard, knowing I intimately care about them and their progressions, even though they often wonder how on earth I get through everything.

No, I do not touch on everything for any one call. Based on the discussion, I normally hit on two or three items that are relevant to that person and will strike a heart cord. I share stories about me, my life, and those whom I infect and affect – and vice versa.

Some tell me I am unique in how I engage with people. While I appreciate the lovely words, I do not believe I am unique. We are all gifted with caring words for our children, siblings, parents, and friends. I just choose to use that same thinking with everyone I meet.

Sure, I have been taken advantage of and a handful of people have been absolute idiots in using my vulnerabilities against me. I experience infinitely more upsides from the people I meet in this space of life than from those individuals. I chose to engage with every human with my whole self. So can you. It is a choice. Battling to buy into the concept? Go read *Unleash the Power Within*[13] - the

---

[13] Unleash the Power Within by Tony Robinsons

choice to be here, deliberate, and fully present is for each of us to make. It is a state of mind.

My Pitch

I help company founders and CEOs who are struggling with scale. This could be with their team, culture, and leadership development, and/or efficient use of time and money. I am also gifted at helping teams decode their CEO.

By intimately personalizing their dream and intent, I help free up time and establish a self-sustaining engine.

What I do

I help inspire individuals, founders, and teams. I am excellent at pulling the best out of people and driving toward a shared consciousness.

My superpower is an intuitive sense of the most efficient path toward outcomes focusing on the best use of time and money. While being able to dive deep, I am an extreme multiplier and make myself redundant as quickly as I can.

I love for and care about people. I am unconventional and humble, and I make myself vulnerable. I am a servant-pleaser and always looking for opportunities to pay it forward.

I am an outstanding facilitator. People experience themselves to be heard, appreciated, accepted, and inspired when they engage with me.

What is your takeaway about me from this small section? What will you remember without having spoken a word with me?

Some Sample Pitches

Depending on the audience, the following are some sample pitches I use.

"I assist Founders and CEOs in cultivating their ideal company culture while optimizing their use of time and financial resources. Through leadership coaching, strategic insights, and practical confidence checks, I help create autonomous teams and a self-sustaining business model, allowing leaders to save time and bypass bureaucratic inefficiencies."

"I support overwhelmed owners and leaders of mid-market companies by clarifying strategic priorities, mobilizing and aligning teams, developing processes and systems, and enhancing leadership capabilities. This results in increased profits, more efficient operations, passionate employees, and a loyal customer base."

"I assist financial leaders in medium and large companies facing challenges with workload and skill gaps by supplying interim accounting and finance experts. These professionals help achieve your strategic goals efficiently."

"I support SaaS and technology companies facing scaling challenges by offering Go-to-Market (GTM) strategies and operational support, leading to a model of repeatable and sustainable growth."

"I assist business owners and leaders in the commercial flooring and construction industries who are challenged with process inefficiencies, team collaboration, and profitability. Through customized consulting services like sales and marketing automation, personality assessments, and strategic facilitation, I drive accelerated growth, enhance team alignment, and prepare organizations for sustained success."

"I support small and medium businesses grappling with complex IT and cybersecurity issues by conducting thorough assessments, identifying vulnerabilities, and developing and implementing remediation plans. This leads to straightforward solutions to previously difficult questions."

"I assist founders unsure about launching their business by offering an entrepreneurship readiness test followed by educational resources. This helps them determine the right path more quickly, increase potential financial returns, and minimize opportunity costs."

"I support large enterprises facing challenges with technical debt and slow product delivery by implementing agile methodologies and transforming product teams through leadership training and coaching. This leads to enhanced product-market fit, quicker time-to-market, and improved customer and business outcomes."

"I assist companies from various sectors who find it challenging to engage with customers in a manner consistent with their brand promise. Through research, analysis, and collaborative solution development, I help create approaches that meet customer expectations, leading to increased engagement with key customer segments, thereby boosting profitability and growth."

"I support small business leaders in aligning their business objectives with employee performance by offering proven HR strategies and practical solutions. This results in tangible outcomes that benefit both the workforce and the business."

"I assist media and entertainment organizations facing challenges in operations, workforce management, and budget control by offering strategic planning, leadership across functions, and innovative solutions. This leads to optimized operations, increased profitability, and the delivery of award-winning content."

"I help sales representatives and CEOs harness the power of imagery to communicate their brand story effectively. Often, the challenge is that their message doesn't resonate with clients' comprehension levels. By supplying custom graphic design marketing tools, I ensure the content is understood quickly and remembered longer. These visuals engage, connect, and motivate clients to collaborate with my clients, thereby boosting revenue."

Volunteering

As you've already seen, I have strong feelings about volunteering my time and talents. The self-awareness, insights, messaging, and growth I have experienced is astounding. I have learned through volunteering what I am truly good at, what people draw into, the most requested topics, and what affects people the most.

As a generalist, narrowing down my most marketable skills has been tricky. Volunteering as a coach, mentor, and advisor has drastically helped me narrow what I market. This is especially useful if you are looking to pivot careers.

There are many forms of volunteer activities you can participate in. My specific inclusion here is making yourself available in your professional space to help transfer knowledge and know-how as a coach, a mentor, and/or an advisor.

Volunteering your time with no probable benefit speaks to character, helps create context, gives additional color to your mind, and offers intent and approach to your professional space. When someone unwraps you – what do they find, and what do you want them to find?

It took a while after registering on ADPList (more on that in the next few pages) to get my first mentees, specifically because I am not technically focused. They came from all over the world, including Iraq, Bulgaria, Rwanda, Kenya, Botswana, the USA, India, the Dominican Republic, Uzbekistan, and Canada to name a few. I focused on leadership development and self-development for accountability-seekers and job-changers.

Personal Value of Volunteering

These sessions are especially interesting when one can engage with the founders around specific topics in their pitch. This allows for interactive, insightful discussions as opposed to a series of questions by a facilitator or an MC forming a monologue. Constructive engagement with the founder is key, and in my experience, the average founder will absorb your time and knowledge like a sponge.

At one particular event, I met the founder of a startup where our engagement resulted in longer-term, pro-bono coaching. What was I to gain – especially in the long run? A lot, it would seem! I learned what my value proposition with a startup was, and how my experience could be harvested to the benefit of other startups.

All these avenues of volunteering helped me understand myself, what I am good at, what people are drawing on, which in turn allowed me to re-gear and refocus myself for my employment pivot.

Every time you volunteer in the professional world, you can position and present yourself. You get to talk about what you can and can't do, what you're skilled at doing, what you love doing, and what you don't like doing. The best part is you are learning from people. And then you're doing it: advising, mentoring, and coaching them and you're listening to yourself talk. This is priceless as you figure out your pivot message and value.

This all helped me understand how I should pivot myself instead of simply looking for the next job. It helped me focus on groups and forums that would become instrumental in my search for my "next" position. It helped me refine my LinkedIn Profile, my pitches, and how I describe what I do.

Types of Mentors

To become a mentor, a coach or an advisor, you'll need to understand what they are and how they differ from each other.

Mentor
A mentor is typically someone with skills, experience, and capabilities in a specific field. The mentor provides guidance, advice, and support to someone less experienced – a mentee. This often happens over a long period with a focus on the overall development of the mentee. Mentorship involves sharing personal experiences and insights, and the mentor helps the mentee navigate career paths while being an accountability soundboard.

Coach
A coach is a professional who works with individuals to help them achieve specific goals (like developing skills, job changes) and improve performance. The relationship is usually structured and short-term in nature; the focus is on measurable outcomes. Coaches use questioning and active listening to help unlock the potential of those they coach.

An Advisor
An advisor offers expert advice and guidance in a specific field. Advisors are often specialists with extensive knowledge and experience, and provide strategic insights, solve problems, and support decision-making; to name a few. The relationship can vary in duration depending on the individual or organization's objectives.

Advisors operate in various business, operational, and functional areas such as finance, education, technology, and healthcare. For example, a financial advisor helps individuals manage their investments and plan for retirement, while a business advisor provides strategic guidance to help companies grow and succeed.

Volunteer Engines

Want to get involved? What follows are some volunteer engines. The onboarding ramp-up window is quite small – it took me about three months to get to the point where I have a relatively constant stream of mentees.

I expect there are many I have missed, please send me any you are working with or find so that I can include it in the next version of this book. Please send any URLs as well.

Sites I Have Used

The following are the platforms I have engaged with thus far.

ADPList (https://app.adplist.org/)
ADPList is a platform that connects professionals with experts for free. They have a paid mentorship option as well, which I have not had anyone sign up for yet. ADPList aims to support career growth acceleration and personal

development by bringing a global community of mentors covering a wide range of soft and hard skills such as design, product management, AI, tech, leadership, and operations. Topics cover mentees looking to build confidence as a leader, grow networks, or define a legacy. Mentees are scattered across the globe.

PushFar (https://www.pushfar.com/home/)

PushFar is a mentoring platform that connects students and professionals with expert mentors to support career growth and personal development. This platform aims to make mentoring accessible to everyone, regardless of their background or experience level, and is dedicated to creating a community through high-quality mentorship and collaboration. There is (at the time of writing this) no paid-option, and mentees are mainly based in Europe and in Africa.

MentorCruise (https://mentorcruise.com/)

MentorCruise is a mentoring platform connecting professionals with expert mentors to support career growth and personal development. MentorCruise provides free and paid options. Topic areas include building confidence as a leader, growing your network, and defining your legacy.

Year Up (https://volunteer.yearup.org/)

Year Up's national workforce training program is designed to empower young adults from underserved communities. Year Up provides them with the skills, experiences, insights, and support. The program focuses on high-demand sectors such as IT and Financial Services. The goal is to assist participants in securing well-paying jobs. Year Up supports the creation of career pathways, real-world internships, personalized coaching, in-person and virtual learning opportunities focusing on high-demand sectors. Year Up is dedicated to ending the opportunity divide and ensuring that every young adult has the chance to achieve their full potential.

TiE (The Indus Entrepreneurs - https://tie.org/)

The Indus Entrepreneurs, or TiE as they are more commonly known, is a global nonprofit organization dedicated to fostering entrepreneurship and supporting startups at all stages of their journey. TiE creates wealth and opportunities through its five programs: Mentoring, Networking, Education, Funding, and Incubation.

Your Average Startup Incubator

It is probable your city has a startup incubator or two nearby. These are great hotbeds for you to get involved with, either through the program or at pitch days where you will hear founders pitch and call for help. These incubators all offer mentoring, networking, educational programs, investor access, offices, communities, and tools.

A Bing, Google, ChatGPT, and CoPilot List

I have included an expanded list of volunteer engines, complete with URLs and descriptions. Take note that while I have looked at each of these, I have not engaged with them directly. If you know of any others – I'm sure there are more out there – please get in touch. I'd be happy to include them in the next edition of this book. If you have experienced any of these platforms and feel they don't deserve to be on this list, I'd love to hear from you as well.

- Big Brothers Big Sisters of America: One-on-one mentoring relationships to help youth achieve their potential through professionally supported programs nationwide.
(https://www.bbbs.org/)
- SCORE: A nationwide American network providing business mentoring for aspiring entrepreneurs.
https://www.score.org/
- MENTOR: An American national effort expanding mentoring relationships for young people. Connects individuals with mentors.
https://www.mentoring.org/
- YMCA: Leadership development, sports, and academic support for young adults.
https://www.ymca.org/
- 4-H: Hands-on learning and leadership for youth across rural, suburban, and urban communities.
https://4-h.org/
- Youth Volunteer Corps: Engages youth (11-18) in service projects to build work and life skills.
https://yvc.org/
- Habitat for Humanity Youth Programs: Help build homes for those in need while fostering civic engagement.
https://www.habitat.org/volunteer/youth-programs
- Camp Fire: Leadership, outdoor experiences, and service projects for youth and young adults.
https://campfire.org/
- VolunteerMatch: Connecting individuals to a wide range of volunteer opportunities based on their interest and location.

https://www.volunteermatch.org/
- Pay It Forward Foundation: Promotes acts of kindness and social responsibility, support for community-led projects.
https://www.payitforwardfoundation.org/
- DoSomething.org: Young people to lead volunteer and pay-it-forward projects on causes they care about.
https://www.dosomething.org/
- YouthBuild USA: Equips young adults with job skills through community-focused construction projects.
https://youthbuild.org/
- Team Rubicon: Disaster response and community resilience projects.
https://teamrubiconusa.org/
- Catchafire: Matches professionals with volunteer projects that fit their skill sets.
https://www.catchafire.org/
- Points of Light: Encourages volunteers to take action in their communities and provide resources for youth engagement.
https://www.pointsoflight.org/
- Serve.gov: Community service with opportunities for people of all backgrounds.
https://www.serve.gov/
- HandsOn Network: Connecting people to meaningful service opportunities.
https://www.handsonnetwork.org/
- Founders Network: A peer mentorship community for tech startup founders; provides support for business growth.

https://foundersnetwork.com/
- GrowthMentor: Growth marketing and product mentors for guidance and advice.
https://www.growthmentor.com/
- Startupbootcamp: Industry-focused startup accelerators providing mentorship, investment, and networking.
https://www.startupbootcamp.org/
- Techstars: Accelerator programs and mentorship for startups, helping entrepreneurs succeed.
https://www.techstars.com
- Y Combinator: Accelerator providing seed funding, mentorship, and support for early-stage companies.
https://www.ycombinator.com
- SCORE Mentors: Business mentoring services to entrepreneurs and small business owners.
https://www.score.org/find-mentor
- Startup Grind: Networking, mentorship, and educational resources.
https://www.startupgrind.com/
- Founder Institute: Pre-seed startup accelerator offering a structured program and mentorship.
https://fi.co/
- MassChallenge: Zero-equity startup accelerator providing mentorship, resources, and networking opportunities.
https://masschallenge.org/
- Coaching Corps: Trains and places volunteer coaches with after-school programs serving low-income communities.
https://www.coachingcorps.org/

- Girls Who Code: Teaching girls to code and providing them with mentorships from professionals in the tech industry.
  https://girlswhocode.com/
- iMentor: Matches students with college-educated mentors to support them through high school, college, and their early careers.
  https://www.imentor.org/
- The Posse Foundation: Leaders from diverse backgrounds gain access to top colleges and universities.
  https://www.possefoundation.org/
- College Possible: Supports low-income students through college admission, enrollment, and completion.
  https://collegepossible.org/
- Management Leadership for Tomorrow: Minorities for leadership roles in business, tech, and nonprofit sectors. Offers personalized coaching and mentorship.
  https://mlt.org/
- The Buddy Program: Mentoring in Colorado (US), pairing children with adult mentors for long-term relationships.
  https://buddyprogram.org/
- The First Tee: Golf as a platform to teach youth life skills, values, and confidence.
  https://www.firsttee.org/
- The Spark Program: Middle school students with hands-on apprenticeships and mentorships to explore careers.
  https://www.sparkprogram.org/

- The National CARES Mentoring Movement: Black adults to mentor black children in underserved communities.
  https://www.caresmentoring.org/
- Boys & Girls Clubs of America: Children and teens focusing on academic success, character, and healthy lifestyles.
  https://www.bgca.org/
- Girl Scouts of the USA: Leadership skills, confidence, and character. Wide range of educational and social activities.
  https://www.girlscouts.org/
- Hispanic Scholarship Fund: Financial aid and mentoring to Hispanic students pursuing higher education.
  https://www.hsf.net/
- Society of Hispanic Professional Engineers (SHPE): Professionals in STEM fields through mentorship, scholarships, and networking events.
  https://www.shpe.org/

STOP – Glance Back at Those

Yes – I know, a bit much – done so by design.

My intent is to tell you that somewhere out there, there is someone who needs to learn what you know, needs your smile, your voice, your hands for something they cannot do or don't have access to.

Go back and look at that list again. Still don't find anything that matches you? Go and google – I promise you will find something. You need to decide – it is out there!

Making LinkedIn Work for You

Trying to Figure Out My Pitch Out

My career saw me regularly switching from business to technology, then back to business usage to understanding technical enablement and constraints. This journey covered banking, mainframes, data-lakes, activity-based costing, business analysis, application development, outsourcing, service improvements, organizational change, business process optimizations, hardware, software and subscription pricing models, sales support, human resources, scale-up and down, project and program management, product management, startups, IP management, logistics, startup technology stabilization, leadership development, financial modeling, revenue modeling, sales, sales support, sales operations, investor messaging, board meeting support, facilitation... A mouth full!

I have worked or consulted in numerous verticals, including banking, reinsurance, oil and gas, education, government, financial, retail, and manufacturing in South Africa, Europe, the UK, the USA, Canada ,and Central America.

My journey has been riddled with fun and laughter while having very little to no structure to it. It has put me in a great position to take a step back from transactional problems or, when I'm speaking and coaching individuals and startups, to look at the bigger picture and not get bogged down with the details or transactions. I have burned my fingers so many times... I am not shy to lean-in on directive opinion and guidance.

This has placed me in what is called the generalist space, where I can do an awful lot, and there is no single bucket I can place my value in. This wide range of skills makes it very hard to "sell" myself on LinkedIn or at networking events; I often fall into explanations bordering on verbal diarrhea when I'm asked, "So, what *do* you do?"

All of this created serious challenges in positioning my LinkedIn profile, what I'm capable of doing, and honing down what I should be focused on. Why would someone hire me? What would they hire me for? Any one skill by itself seemed irrelevant, and any combination would be relevant to some and irrelevant to others.

My last salaried employment saw me at a company where I eventually filled the role of Chief Operations Officer responsible for everything non-product operation specific. This included everything around business operations such as IP, leases, contracts, scale-up, scale-down, HR policies, benefits, QA, marketing, sales, the data lab, and all of the supporting functions making sure the other units' divisions could get their work done.

When the news in March 2024 brought with it the dire need to pivot, I saw my world crumbling. I knew I was in trouble. I may have said some bad words before the questions came: "What do I do with myself now?" and "What is my pitch?" and "Where do I start?" I realized my network was old, and I needed to decide how I would reengage with them, all the while wondering who would care to help and, quite honestly, what the hell I was going to do.

To Automate or Not

Like nearly everyone I've spoken to, I started using LinkedIn manually. I was actively anti-automation; human connection is a deliberate, intentional, caring, meaningful act – I was in no way going to pass off this important function to tools.

I started researching companies and individual people – covering their backgrounds, missions, value propositions, and causes. I sent personalized messages, spending hours crafting unique, enticing, and caring messages. I found the response rate of about 20% fair and acceptable. I reached out to people I knew and slowly branched out. Initially, I contacted people within my network that I expected would respond – I needed guidance on how on earth to find myself again. I hoped that they would tell me how I should market myself, and where.

20% does not sound like a bad ratio until you measure it against time. Reading up on someone, tracking down what they were doing, what their companies were about, how these companies had grown and how those people had progressed through the company took about 15 minutes. For 20 people, that's at least five hours of work. To have only four people respond – and hopefully have at least one person agree to a meeting – was not economical.

I quickly realized that the hours of work to do these deep, reflective outreaches wouldn't be scalable. It surprised me how few people responded – not knowing the statistics, I expected more would have engaged. I put effort into personalizing the connection request, yet the ratio remained the same. I needed to rethink this. My brain is naturally wired to find inefficiencies and maximize outcomes.

One of the people I met told me about LinkedIn campaigns. They were trying to sell me on how they could get me hot leads and fill my calendar; told me I simply needed to close the deals. They wanted $3,000 up front and a monthly fee of $800 – for meetings. Probing, I figured out they were using a mix of automation and human contact.

I learned the secret behind this is pure numbers. I needed to find a quick way to eliminate the 16 non-responsive people from every 20 I was contacting. The diligent time and care I was putting into these 16 people was simply not productive.

What ensued are the ratios I referenced earlier. Using the tools for three months resulted in a false start, and then I figured it out. A four-month average of 690 outreaches in a month converted to 218 connections, which converted to about 80 meetings, either via video or face-to-face. In four months, my network grew by 3,586 people, but most importantly, I had about 440 people regularly communicating with me – some significantly more than others.

Let's reverse this conversion and discover the manual hours it would have taken to achieve this outcome: Assuming a maximum of 10 minutes were spent per outreach – just the initial outreach to get to these great outcomes I have – that's 35,860 minutes or almost 600 hours dedicated to just the initial contacts. Running this manually is just not scalable.

The outcomes and results I have experienced thus far speak of expansive networking:

- I've developed a good number of friends,
- I have found at least 30+ life-changing websites,
- I've been introduced to eight professional forums I had no idea existed,
- I joined the Atlanta Executive Network,
- I met CEOs, authors, and angel investors I would not ever have found,
- I became an author,
- I've mentored dozens of people across the globe, including founders to help them find their feet and passion,
- I've engaged in the Atlanta founder and VC community,
- And I finally became physically active.

It's a Numbers Game

Getting to the people who will buy your time or service is a sheer numbers and ratio game. The more compelling your message, the simpler it will be to get to your targets; this applies to products and services.

Let's make the number relevant to what we used to do before Covid and LinkedIn. We attended conferences. Pick a conference in your vertical of specialty skill set, be it CRMs, Salesforce, enterprise software, engineering, space, video games, Comic-Con, CES, basketball. Any. At any event, there will be at least 2,000 attendees over a four-day event.

Given you have a booth at the conference, or you are someone who visits booths at the event, it is not probable for you to meet more than 40 people a day, resulting in 160 business cards. From those 160 business cards, you will probably end up engaging with about 16 of those people after the conference and probably do business with three or four people.

What you are not seeing is for those 2,000 people to attend, there are probably some 10,000 to 20,000 people who would want to attend if they had the time and money. Further to this: There are probably 100,000 to 200,000 people in the industry directly relevant to the conference.

Your business opportunity is – thinking conservatively – about four people out of 100,000 – and YOU must find those four people without knowing who they are or having access to them at a conference. They sure as heck are not going to come to you or me without a significant amount of work.

This is exactly what I attempt to cover below, using LinkedIn as your initiation point of entry to your networking and lead generation efforts.

Tools List

There are some basic categories of tools you will need.

LinkedIn – the professional gravity point. For you to access the benefits of the system you will need to upgrade to LinkedIn Premium if you have not yet.

LinkedIn Sales Navigator is designed for sales professionals, with advanced search capabilities, lead recommendations, profile tracking, and CRM integrations. It provides personalized account and leads suggestions, InMail messaging, and detailed insights into buying committees.

Campaign Automation tools are LinkedIn automation tools that are used to create custom sales funnels, automating connection requests, profile views, messages, and likes. They typically provide analytics for performance tracking, all while prioritizing user account safety with cloud-based technology. They range from being free through to monthly recurring and annual fees. Some have steep learning curves; some are very simple to use and may include integration into your chosen CRM. Tools include Dux-Soup, Dripify, Expandi, Octopus CRM, Salesflow, Meet Alfred, and LinkedRadar to name a few.

Customer Relationship Management (CRM) tools are software designed to help manage and analyze interactions with current and potential customers, centralizing data like contact information, purchase history, customer communications, customer retention, sales growth, and streamlining marketing and sales processes. Some examples include HubSpot CRM, Salesforce, Zoho CRM, Freshsales, Zendesk Sell, Microsoft Dynamics 365, ClickUp, Keap, NetSuite CRM+, and Bitrix24.

Calendaring tools offer automated scheduling where users share their availability through customizable booking pages while integrating with their calendars on platforms like Google and Outlook. They provide features such as setting meeting types, automated reminders, time zone conversions, payment processing, and CRM integrations. Examples include Doodle, Acuity Scheduling, Cal.com, Squarespace Scheduling, Calendly, TidyCal, Setmore, Zoho Bookings, SimplyBook.me, Book Like A Boss, and HubSpot Meetings to name a few.

Spreadsheet automation tools allow for record manipulation, merging, extraction, and list creation. Many of these tools are built to help you. They could constrict how you can extract and focus. You will regularly end up exporting, merging, and dropping new lists back into your automation tool.

Pure Automation Will Fail - Quickly

I had a false start in using automation. I had four campaigns running when I first onboarded these tools. Two of them yielded me a 6% connection rate and a 1% response rate. The other two yielded me a 32% connection rate and a 21% response rate – remarkably higher.

After speaking to a few people, it became clear to me that I was positioning and selling in two of the campaigns and giving and serving on the other two. No guess which two campaigns were yielding results and networking!

Once I realized that campaigns focus around giving and serving yielded the better results, I deleted and reset the campaigns and started again which has resulted in the outcomes described here.

Automation is NOT about automating and walking away. If you do this, you will just end up in the spam bucket. I have to date had about 14 people ask to be unsubscribed, and about 16 people remove me as a connection.

You have to find a healthy balance between using tools and developing your funnel through human, caring, hands-on activities.

Automation Can Land to Being Banned

Disclaimer: I have no idea how the LinkedIn algorithms work, or what gets you reviewed vs banned. I strongly recommend absolute caution, and care to be progressive, engaged, mindful, and deliberate as you leverage the platform.

LinkedIn is looking for human engagement. The more consistently you engage there – by reacting to and commenting on posts, and creating posts of your own – the less chance you have of being tagged for jail.

This means using automation judiciously and slowly increasing its utilization. Most automation tools have settings to help limit your exposure to being banned – I strongly recommend you stay within their rules and guidance.

I suggest you vary your involvement. Switch between posting, browsing, messaging, responding, and automation. Do as much as you can to create variation – different messages, different windows of time, differing and random actions.

Take Your Campaign Beyond LinkedIn

LinkedIn and automation are only the lead identification part of your business development journey. Once you have your engaged list of names and opportunities, you will need to develop relationships with them that make you memorable and will result in the movement of money.

Effective relationships will end up in people challenging you to tell your stories and even write books. They will present you with technologies, software, websites, and processes you could never have thought of and probably would never have found by yourself.

They will introduce you to people who you would not have thought to contact. They will invite you into forums and bodies of people you did not know existed or would not have had the ability to penetrate.

They will challenge how you sell yourself, how you show up, and how you speak about what you do. They will encourage you to attend networking events and conferences you never imagined existed, and they will – almost daily – open a horizon of new possibilities.

You must be prepared for this and be ready to engage. What follows in the pages ahead is how I have managed to leverage these tools to find my list of people who have affected my life, and who have yielded these values for me.

Good hunting! And please, let me know what did and did not work for you. I would love to publish an updated version of this book in my desire to keep paying it forward.

LinkedIn Automation

The LinkedIn Bar

LinkedIn is the digital, 24/7 version of you meeting someone at a conference or networking event. At a conference, bar, or networking event you would simply not walk up to someone and blurt out "Hi, I sell services to help you figure out your leadership strategy," and immediately elaborate on why you've done this in similar companies, saving them thousands. Surely you won't end by saying "I am available to answer any questions you have," and then wait for their response in anticipation.

I would not walk up to you and say "My name is Andrew, I am great at working with people, I have helped them solve complex problems, saving time and money. I have references and a track record of impacting companies. I use a structured process and methodology."

Your mindset has to see LinkedIn as a digital conference. You need to stop selling. Just STOP.

How would you want to be approached at a networking event you attended? This is how you should start. The first thing you would probably do is walk up to someone and say "Hey, my name is Andrew, I don't believe we have met".

High-Level Approach

My approach is stupidly simple, common sense really – it just takes time and patience. While developing your network, don't ask for anything, references, positions, jobs, opportunities, and do not "position" yourself. Your LinkedIn profile should brag about your message, not you.

This is my process:

- Find people who want to be met in the LinkedIn Bar.
- Figure out what they, their company, and their profession like, do, and follow.
- Engage with the person by giving provocative, insightful messages that provoke a response, and then speak with them.
- Develop a relationship with them, pay an interest, help them.
- When they want to meet, offer them a simple way to book your time.
- Meet with them with a focus on learning who they are while making myself memorable.
- Stay in touch and introduce them to similar people who can assist them, or people they can assist.

Engagement and Time

Manage your time and energy. A working campaign should take four to six weeks before you experience momentum. It will take three to four months before you have a decent engagement rate with your ideal network.

Be patient, don't rush it, and allow the process to run. You will see a slow uptick in people asking to speak and engage with you. Manage the volume of touchpoints so that you don't affect your salaried job too heavily.

LinkedIn is a lead generator, not your whole campaign. You must make sure to balance the LinkedIn campaign with forums, networking, volunteer work, and your postings – be it LinkedIn, X, Instagram, Facebook, etc.

Getting your Target Profiles

Your first important task is getting a sound, relevant list of possible connections. This is called your Ideal Customer Profile (ICP).

Your ICP list is built for the campaign you want to launch. I have about eight campaigns running at any given time, focusing on old contacts, new fractional executives, CEOs, etc. Each campaign has different constructs and reasons for running. They all have the same target outcome – getting someone to engage. Whether it is them just saying "hi" back at you, or agreeing to meet you, or review your book.

Things that may influence your ICP list include[14]:

- Job title
- Years in position
- Years at company
- Last job change
- Company name

---

[14] Email me for a copy of the presentation with some samples. I will have the website up soon, www.youdecide.us where you will be able to download this.

- Vertical
- What is their country, state, city location
- When last were they active on LinkedIn
- Are they a first-, second- or third-degree contact?

This is where Sales Navigator is worth the money you pay to leverage the service. It drastically reduces the number of profiles in your ICP list. The advanced search functionality is an absolute game-changer, whether you are using it manually, or as a hybrid of automation tools and manual activities and engagements.

Depending on the automation tools you use, you will copy your search query in, copy LinkedIn Profile URLs, or upload CSV files with Profile URLs.

Your goal is to have this list as focused and specific as you can. Every name on the list matters. Why? Whether you are looking to contact 600 or 6,000 people in your search for a specific customer, your ICP query list will run each of the profiles through your campaign. A poorly built ICP list will cause significant delays in reaching your target audience. Reducing the ICP list to a very specific profile will help you narrow your message, reduce how long it takes to get through the list and have a high probability of finding the profiles that matter.

Remember - It's a Numbers Game

The number of connections you have now comes into play. The more relevant connections you have, the more second and third-degree connections you will be able to access in your ICP list.

Assume each person has 10 connections – that means your search limit is confined to 1,000 profiles in total. If each person has 100 connections, you'll have access to one million users in total. At 200 connections per profile, you will have access to some 5 million profiles.

On average LinkedIn profiles have about 930 contacts. Let's assume, for simplicity's sake, that connections are capped at 100. If you have 100 connections, your total search capacity will be limited to 1 million profiles. If you have 5,000 connections, that changes to 50 million possible profiles.

Catch-22: The key to a good ICP list is getting it down to as small a concise targeted list as you can. That means the 50 million possible profiles work against you since the automation tool will start at the top of the list and randomly work its way through the list you feed it. Assume you can (for LinkedIn Jail reasons) only process 100 profiles in a week, and your ICP list includes 3,000 profiles, the campaign will only be completed in 30 weeks.

3,000 profiles may be a valid list, just know it will take 30 weeks to get through it. The key is using a targeted list so that every profile being processed is worth the clock time. Keep in mind that, although you are only going to yield a small percentage of those 3,000 as potential customers, this is only one campaign!

Automation Campaigns

Campaigns Explained

A campaign is a feature available in one of the tools referenced above that allows you to create a set of steps. These are instructions that the tool executes on your behalf, as if it were you, to the ICP list over a specified time.

In English, a campaign allows you to tell the tool to execute a set of steps you would have done manually. An example is:

- Step 1: View the profile
- Step 2 after 1 hour: Like a post
- Step 3 after 7 days: View the profile
- Step 4 after 3 days: View the profile
- Step 5 after 1 hour: Request a connection
- Step 6 after accepting: Say thank you for connecting
- Step 7 after 4 days: Send a message
- Step 8 after 6 days: View profile

What the automation does is takes your ICP list and, one at a time, process the contacts through the steps above. This means if you have a list of 100 Profiles in your ICP it takes #1 and does step 1, then moves that one to step 2. While it is processing profile #1 it starts profile #2 and then follows the same steps. It then starts #3, and #4 and so on until all the steps slowly populate with profiles executing at different stages – within the limitations of keeping you out of LinkedIn Jail.

The magic of automation, and staying within their rules, allows you to automatically engage in a way that has a low probability of landing you in LinkedIn Jail for overuse, abuse, or breaching the terms of service and use agreement of the LinkedIn platform. This campaign runs within the work hours you allocate, i.e., 9 to 5 PM, five days a week, and runs without you being involved.

You will see that Steps 1, 2, 3, 4, and 8 are all soft touches. These steps have no action other than creating an engagement history on the profile that informs the person I pay attention to him, her, or them.

I often have people reach out proactively, saying they saw I viewed their profile and asking how they can help. It signals to the person I am not just "making a sales call" as I have been engaged with their profile for a while.

I hear you saying this is devious as I am not really looking at the profile. Remember the ratios here: 16 profiles you do view out of 20 will not know you looked at them. Your objective here is to try drive engagement.

The following are some example campaigns.

Campaign Message Fundamentals

The messages you send, whether to ask to connect, say thank you, introduce people, pass information, or give insights, should be of a complete giving nature.

Don't offer your services or goods to avoid coming across as self-promoting or selling. Do not brag about how good you are or about being available, and do not ask for a job, or if that person knows anyone hiring.

If you are at that stage of desperation, you should reach out to, and only to, people whom you know incredibly well and have a deep, known relationship with. Any "blast from the past" or cavalier outreach of this kind is bound to get your message deleted and feed further into your despondency and desperation.

Take the time now to develop your network and outreach campaign while you are not under pressure or desperate. Take sound, calm, deliberate time to build intentional relationships – and start now.

Make sure your messages are personalized, even if they are automated, and make sure they are wickedly relevant to your target ICP. Every messages should be focused on serving your ICP. You want to give, serve, inform, and offer insight.

When someone asks what you do, don't ramble on about how smart you are and everything you are capable of. Answer questions in rich brevity. Allow them to probe you. Answer in ways that invite further discussion, be this written or auditory. Always drive the discussions with values and outcomes as opposed to skills and capabilities.

I have included a few example campaigns below that I've used in my fractional world. In addition, there are examples for a software developer, a vinyl pressor's small business, and a machinist. I have taken stabs at example messages and expect it might generate a good chuckle or two from people in those professions. Please reach out to me – I look forward to the next version of this book where I'd happily include some more realistic examples.

Example 1: Existing Contacts

This campaign is focused on existing contacts and seeks to re-strike relations and communications with them.

For each of the four professions, Steps 1, 2, and 4 are similar – they are all focused on profile engagement activities. Steps 3, 5, and 6 – where messages are sent – will be distinct based on your profession; I've included example messages listed in four threads.

The key is to be human, intentional, and vulnerable. I'd suggest leveraging no more than three or four automated messages since you might quickly be viewed (or worse – flagged!) as spam. Your aim should be to show a deliberate intent to engage with the person without asking for anything.

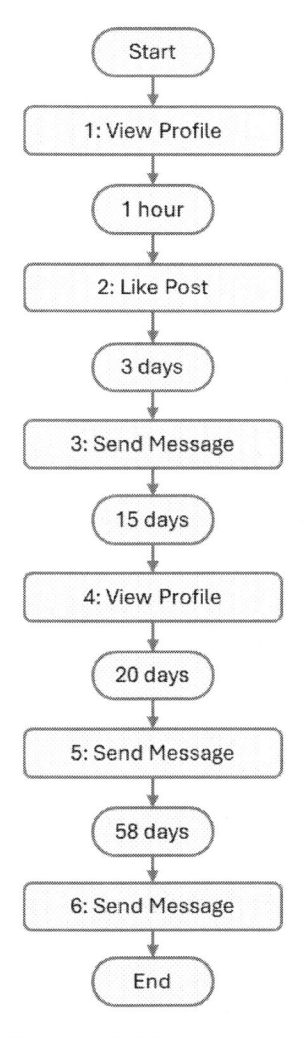

```
Start
  ↓
1: View Profile
  ↓
1 hour
  ↓
2: Like Post
  ↓
3 days
  ↓
3: Send Message
  ↓
15 days
  ↓
4: View Profile
  ↓
20 days
  ↓
5: Send Message
  ↓
58 days
  ↓
6: Send Message
  ↓
End
```

Thread 1: My Outreach

Step 3's Message:
> "If you have not heard I am venturing back into the consulting world (as a Fractional Executive) where I am merging my consulting and executive experiences ("Fractional" being part-time executive). I continue to be involved in LifeQ and driving the vision.
>
> My focus in the fractional world is helping fractured leadership teams (executives all the way down) as well as driving efficient use of resources (people, time, and money). In this fractional space I am currently mixing with hundreds of executives, some amazing people across the exec suite – talk about fire-hose learnings!
>
> Would love to catch up – I have been remiss as I have been heads down keeping my world spinning."

Note: I am delivering THREE pieces of core information here, the most important being the last.

- Pivoting my career,
- Expressing interest to re-establish contact,
- And extending apologies for not staying in touch.

Step 5's Message:
> "Three books I could not help but share:

Regardless of your position and pitch I recommend you read 10x Is Easier than 2x *by Dan Sullivan & Benjamin Hardy.*

New Sales. Simplified by Mike Weinberg is great if you are looking to refresh you pitch message

And a very interesting, pragmatic read on pitching anything – your services, selling your goods, your company, or your ideas is Pitch Anything *by Oren Klaff.*

I'm always growing my list; please shoot me any titles you regard highly."

Note: I am ...

- Not asking for anything.
- Giving information.
- Trying to draw in discussion.

Step 6's Message:
"It's been an interesting few months. Outside of networking and job hunting, I have also sat down to author three books.

- Leading Magnanimously *will be available in February and launches in August.*
- You Decide: Own and Drive your Referrals, Relationships and Reputation *– using LinkedIn. My goal is to have this done in the coming 4 to 6 weeks.*

- *Hope is a Powerful Emotion; a 'names and places have been changed' book where I became truly American and ended up suing someone. I hope to have this book done in the next 3 or 6 months.*

Never a dull moment :)

I trust you are well. Let me know if you want me to get you a copy of these non-fiction books. E-books are easy; paperbacks can be arranged with shipping costs."

Note: I am ...

- Not asking for anything.
- Giving information.
- Trying to draw in discussion.

Thread 2: Software Developer

Step 3's Message:

"If you haven't heard, I've been diving deeper into the tech world and have progressed from Python development into machine learning. I am now advancing into the fascinating field of AI. This has allowed me to merge my technical expertise with my passion for solving complex problems.

While I remain involved in my current projects – driving innovation and execution – I've been focused on building solutions that leverage AI to deliver meaningful impact. The past few months have been a whirlwind of learning and growth.

I'd love to catch up and hear what's new with you. Apologies for being out of touch – things have been intense as I've been heads-down pushing boundaries!

Looking forward to reconnecting soon."

Step 5's Message:

"Three books I could not help but share.

For those diving into AI, Deep Learning *by Ian Goodfellow, Yoshua Bengio, and Aaron Courville is a foundational read.*

A fantastic approach to foster a problem-solving mindset is Grokking Algorithms *by Aditya Bhargava.*

For a deeper look at the ethical and societal implications of AI, check out Human Compatible *by Stuart Russell.*

I'm always growing my list – please shoot me titles any you regard highly!"

Step 6's Message:

"Have you seen the Verge article on what's happening with AI talent right now? All out to recruit top AI researchers. There are only some 1,000 people capable of developing the latest models.

https://www.theverge.com/2024/12/20/24326135/ai-talent-wars-databricks-interview

The money going into AI is ridiculous, OpenAI's 18-month Orion project's costs are already hitting half a billion dollars!

https://www.wsj.com/tech/ai/openai-gpt5-orion-delays-639e7693

Curious to know what you are seeing!"

Thread 3: Small Business

Step 3's Message:
"If you haven't heard, my small vinyl pressing business has been evolving fantastically, growing into something much larger than I could have estimated. We've recently had the opportunity to work with some relatively well-known musicians and are now expanding our reach into neighboring states.

This journey has been and continues to be challenging, to put it mildly. So many lessons learned. Balancing the creative and operational sides of the business has been a whirlwind.

I'd love to catch up and hear what's been happening with you. Apologies for not staying in touch – it's been a busy time as we've focused on taking it to the next level!

Looking forward to reconnecting soon."

Step 5's Message:
"Three books I could not help but share.

Profit First *by Mike Michalowicz has been a game-changer for me in managing finances effectively.*

The E-Myth Revisited *by Michael E. Gerber was essential for understanding how to scale from a boutique operation to a larger enterprise.*

And for creative and branding insights, This Is Marketing *by Seth Godin gave me some incredible 'in plain sight' nuggets.*

I'm always growing my list – please shoot me titles any you regard highly!"

Step 6's Message:
"You'll love this. The Tennessean *talked about this new place in Nashville called The Vinyl Lab. It's a live music venue that also presses records! What a creative blend of music and manufacturing. Inspiring does not begin to describe this – watch this space.*

https://www.tennessean.com/story/entertainment/music/2024/12/18/nashville-vinyl-lab-records-dolly-parton-guns-n-roses/74972199007/."

Thread 4: Machinist

Step 3's Message:

"If you haven't heard, my career in machining has taken an exciting turn! You will recall me being in the Midwest honing my skills with lathes, CNCs, and mills. Well – I did it, relocated to Texas, and stepped into a management position. What a transition.

The move has been a whirlwind; I'm excited about the opportunities ahead and the chance to make an impact on this little city.

I'd love to catch up and hear what's been happening in your world. Apologies for being out of touch – between learning the ropes in management and settling into Texas, things have been moving fast!

Looking forward to reconnecting soon."

Step 5's Message:

"Three books I could not help but share.

I found The Goal: A Process of Ongoing Improvement *by Eliyahu M. Goldratt a great foundation as I stepped into management; an operational efficiency must-read.*

The Lean Startup by Eric Ries offers excellent lessons on iterative processes and innovation.

And in the space of leadership – well – when you read this, you will chuckle at how much I needed this. It's called Leaders Eat Last *by Simon Sinek.*

I'm always growing my list – please shoot me titles any you regard highly!"

Step 6's Message:

"Seems automation and robotics are game-changers for CNC machining. It's like the future of manufacturing is already here. Check this out:

https://www.fictiv.com/articles/the-future-of-cnc-machining-2024-and-beyond?

Some interesting trends from BlueBay – demand in aerospace and defense is booming. Feels like we are getting back to the cutting edge!

https://www.bluebayautomation.com/blog/welding-metals-13/cnc-machining-trends-to-watch-in-2024-69

What's your take on this?"

Many people, if not most, in your network will not respond. Leave them, focus on those that do.

Example 2: A Forum You Form Part of

A forum is a group of people you can join that form relatively safe spaces built on common ground or shared interest by its members. This could be sports teams, professional groups, or volunteer groups.

From my journey map earlier in this book, you would have noticed that most of my success has been driven by a professional group of people – one group in particular: Fractionals United.

An example campaign focused on networking with contacts from forums might look like this:

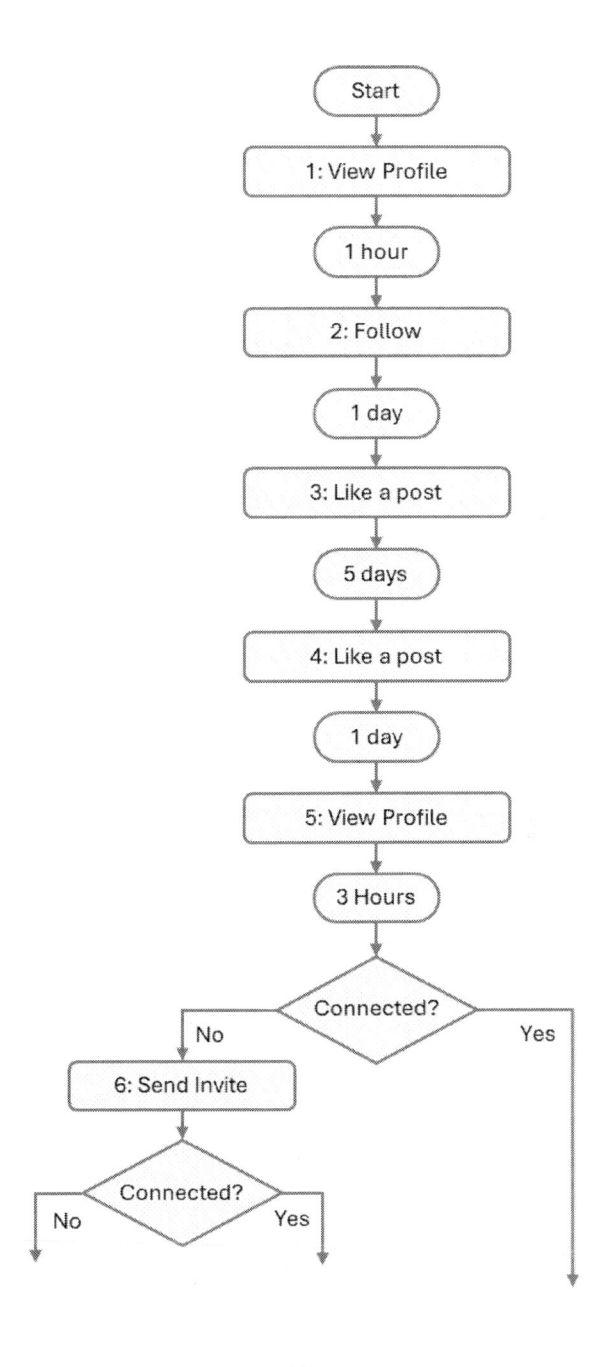

```
Start
  ↓
1: View Profile
  ↓
1 hour
  ↓
2: Follow
  ↓
1 day
  ↓
3: Like a post
  ↓
5 days
  ↓
4: Like a post
  ↓
1 day
  ↓
5: View Profile
  ↓
3 Hours
  ↓
Connected?
  — No → 6: Send Invite → Connected? → No / Yes
  — Yes →
```

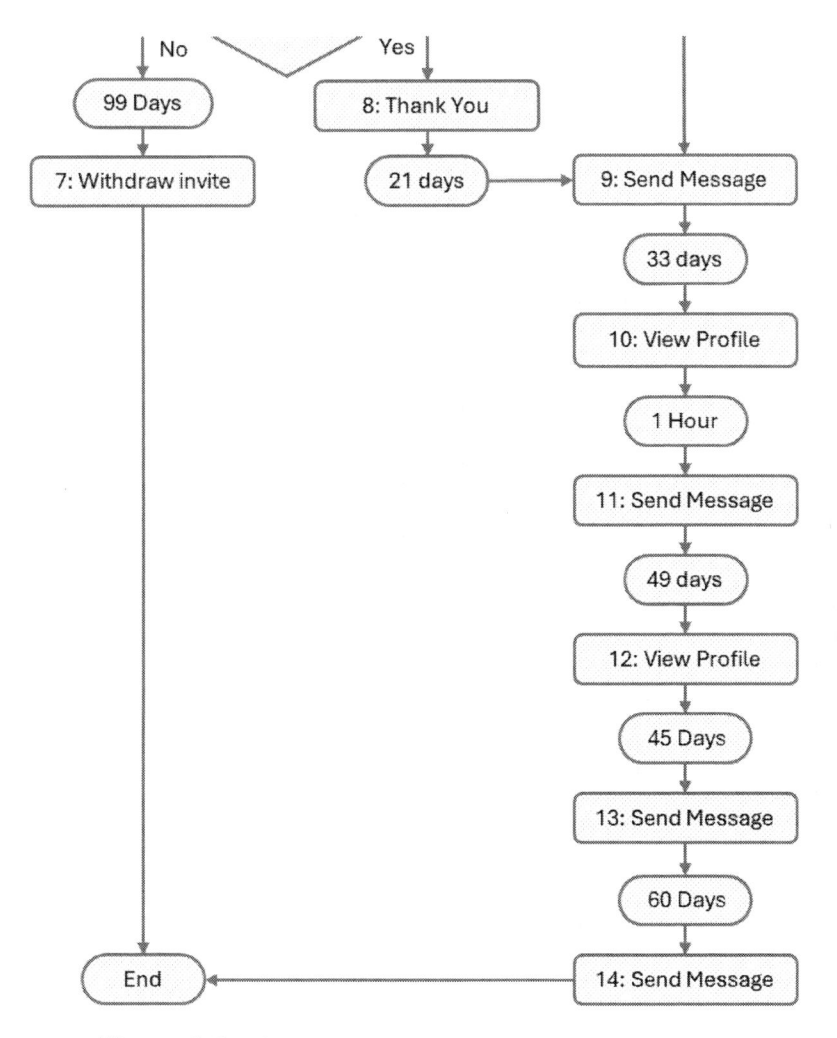

```
        No              Yes
         ↓               ↓
    ┌─────────┐    ┌───────────┐
    │ 99 Days │    │8: Thank You│
    └─────────┘    └───────────┘
         ↓               ↓
 ┌──────────────┐  ┌─────────┐     ┌────────────────┐
 │7: Withdraw invite│  │21 days │ ──→ │9: Send Message │
 └──────────────┘  └─────────┘     └────────────────┘
                                           ↓
                                      ┌─────────┐
                                      │ 33 days │
                                      └─────────┘
                                           ↓
                                   ┌────────────────┐
                                   │10: View Profile│
                                   └────────────────┘
                                           ↓
                                      ┌────────┐
                                      │ 1 Hour │
                                      └────────┘
                                           ↓
                                   ┌────────────────┐
                                   │11: Send Message│
                                   └────────────────┘
                                           ↓
                                      ┌─────────┐
                                      │ 49 days │
                                      └─────────┘
                                           ↓
                                   ┌────────────────┐
                                   │12: View Profile│
                                   └────────────────┘
                                           ↓
                                      ┌─────────┐
                                      │ 45 Days │
                                      └─────────┘
                                           ↓
                                   ┌────────────────┐
                                   │13: Send Message│
                                   └────────────────┘
                                           ↓
                                      ┌─────────┐
                                      │ 60 Days │
                                      └─────────┘
                                           ↓
         ┌─────┐                     ┌────────────────┐
         │ End │ ←─────────────────  │14: Send Message│
         └─────┘                     └────────────────┘
```

The following steps represent engagement interaction: 1, 2, 3, 4, 5, 7, 10, and 12. Again, I'll demonstrate with examples from the four professions used above.

Thread 1, 2, 3, and 4

Step 6 – Send Invite:
   *"Found you in the [**forum**] world. Thank you for connecting!"*

   You can change [forum] to any group you are part of and targeting.

Note: I am ...

- Not asking for anything.
- Assuming the person will connect.

What about pending connections? At the date of publication, I have about 1,700 pending connection invites that are being ignored. In 60 days, these invitations will automatically be withdrawn. You will have yours – just leave them.

Step 8 – Thank You:
   *"Thanks for connecting to a [**forum**] peer! Please let me know how I can serve you."*

Note: I am ...

- Not asking for anything.
- Just saying "THANK YOU".

Thread 1: My Outreach

Step 9's Message:
"Three books I could not help but share:

Regardless of your position and pitch I recommend you read 10x Is Easier than 2x by Dan Sullivan & Benjamin Hardy.

New Sales. Simplified by Mike Weinberg is great if you are looking to refresh you pitch message

And a very interesting, pragmatic read on pitching anything – your services, selling your goods, your company, or your ideas is Pitch Anything by Oren Klaff.

I'm always growing my list; please shoot me any titles you regard highly."

Note: I am …

- Reusing another campaign's text.
- Not asking for anything.
- Giving information.
- Trying to draw in discussion.

Step 11's Message:
"I have good responses here on LinkedIn, and I am using it to build and expand my network and pay it forward. I have a few fractionals who have asked to be included in training sessions.

Please let me know if I should include you in one of the sessions - they are ad hoc.

In summary, I am meeting about 16 new faces every week. I have an upward of 40% connection rate and 25% engagement rate. I have met some incredible people where we have gotten to know one another as humans, not just Zoom characters. I don't think I have found a silver bullet, but there's definitely a silver lining for me. Happy happy to share."

Note: I am …

- Offering knowledge and insights.
- Not asking for anything.
- Not selling.

Step 13's Message:

"FRAK published a pretty informative fractional report for 2024 that is worth reading. Some interesting data:

- *100k+ fractionals*
- *59% are between 44 and 59 years old*
- *12% earn over $250k a year, 30% earn <$50k per year*
- *83% of people go fractional because of flexibility*

And a whole bunch more.

State of Fractional Industry Report, Summer 2024 – read it here: *https://frak.ck.page/02b4cb388e"*

Note: I am …

- Offering knowledge and insights.
- Not asking for anything.
- Not selling.

Thread 2: Software Developer

Step 9's Message:
"Three books I could not help but share.

For those diving into AI, Deep Learning *by Ian Goodfellow, Yoshua Bengio, and Aaron Courville is a foundational read.*

A fantastic approach to foster a problem-solving mindset is Grokking Algorithms *by Aditya Bhargava.*

For a deeper look at the ethical and societal implications of AI, check out Human Compatible *by Stuart Russell.*

I'm always growing my list – please shoot me titles any you regard highly!"

Step 11's Message:
"This 'Emergent Coding' thing seems to be taking off. The decentralized development paradigm is properly challenging current development frameworks. The upfront work is

not insignificant; however, the downstream benefits are astronomical. We are seeing component adoption and an interesting dynamic in specialization and collaboration. The reverse integration and marketplace model are causing us to re-tool a good number of skills – I am in the middle of helping our dev team specialize in niche areas. Would love to bend your ear on what you are seeing ahead of us."

Step 13's Message:
"Combining systematic innovation methods with agile practices seems to offer a structured flexible development approach. What are your thoughts on the introduction of problem-solving and efficient project management to adapt swiftly to market changes and user feedback? I am curious if you have any insights or views on TRIZ or design thinking – specifically for startups."

Thread 3: Small Business

Step 9's Message:
"Three books I could not help but share.

Profit First by Mike Michalowicz has been a game-changer for me in managing finances effectively.

The E-Myth Revisited by Michael E. Gerber was essential for understanding how to scale from a boutique operation to a larger enterprise.

And for creative and branding insights, This Is Marketing *by Seth Godin gave me some incredible 'in plain sight' nuggets.*

I'm always growing my list – please shoot me titles any you regard highly!"

Step 11's Message:
"Advancements in digital recording technology have significantly improved the sound quality of vinyl records. This is part of what is making a difference for us.

By recording music digitally and then transferring it to vinyl, artists can achieve clarity and detail previously unattainable, blending analog warmth with digital precision. This is further amplified through HD for Vinyl.

We are currently investigating digital audio workstation tools including Pro Tools, Logic Pro, and Cubase. Do you have any exposure to these utilities?"

Step 13's Message:
"We have been on a journey of environmentally eco-friendly materials and processes. We have had some exposure to the Australian band Lime Cordiale who collaborated with Brisbane's Suitcase Records and the release of an album using a bio-vinyl process

reducing carbon emissions by 92%. Do you have any insights or references on this trend and technology?"

Thread 4: Machinist

Step 9's Message:

"Three books I could not help but share.

I found The Goal: A Process of Ongoing Improvement by Eliyahu M. Goldratt a great foundation as I stepped into management; an operational efficiency must-read.

The Lean Startup by Eric Ries offers excellent lessons on iterative processes and innovation.

And in the space of leadership – well – when you read this, you will chuckle at how much I needed this. It's called Leaders Eat Last by Simon Sinek.

I'm always growing my list – please shoot me titles any you regard highly!"

Step 11's Message:

"Pressing AI into smart factories underpinned with industry 4.0 principles is changing my world fast. This IOT thing is happening faster than I expected. High-Speed Machining helps to optimize tool paths and cut *speeds, reducing cycle times. This is all very exciting. The unplanned consequences are raw material sourcing and misaligned component delivery for final assembly.*

Are you tracking this evolution? It seems to be changing faster than I can keep up with."

Step 13's Message:
"Further to my last note, **AI and Machine Learning** *integration into CNC machining allows for real-time monitoring and optimization of my processes. This has enabled predictive maintenance, adaptive control, and improved decision-making, reducing downtime and injuries.*

Our improvement ratios seem slightly ahead of market predictions. Wanted to pass on where I have kicked a toe or two and figured out some neat techniques. Let me know if you have a few minutes to chat."

Example 3: Locating an ICP

This campaign follows the same steps as Example 2 above, only the messages differ. And as before, we're not asking, selling, pitching, or positioning ourselves.

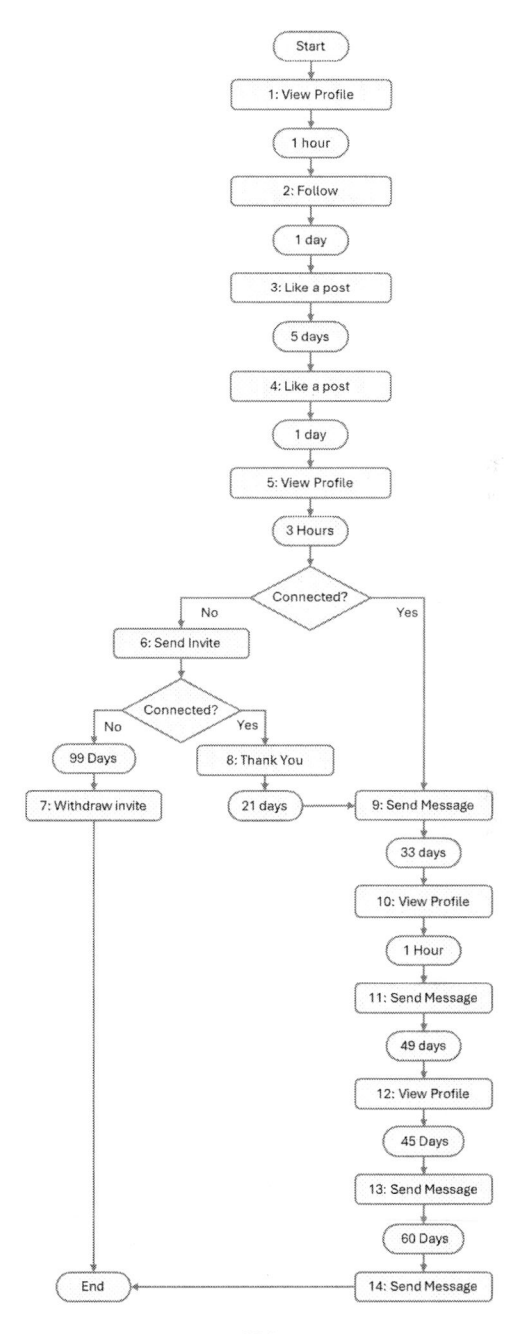

```
Start
  ↓
1: View Profile
  ↓
1 hour
  ↓
2: Follow
  ↓
1 day
  ↓
3: Like a post
  ↓
5 days
  ↓
4: Like a post
  ↓
1 day
  ↓
5: View Profile
  ↓
3 Hours
  ↓
Connected?
 ├── No ──→ 6: Send Invite
 │            ↓
 │          Connected?
 │           ├── No ──→ 99 Days ──→ 7: Withdraw invite ──→ End
 │           └── Yes ─→ 8: Thank You ──→ 21 days ──→ 9: Send Message
 └── Yes ─────────────────────────────────────────────→ 9: Send Message
                                                          ↓
                                                        33 days
                                                          ↓
                                                     10: View Profile
                                                          ↓
                                                        1 Hour
                                                          ↓
                                                     11: Send Message
                                                          ↓
                                                        49 days
                                                          ↓
                                                     12: View Profile
                                                          ↓
                                                        45 Days
                                                          ↓
                                                     13: Send Message
                                                          ↓
                                                        60 Days
                                                          ↓
                                                     14: Send Message
                                                          ↓
                                                         End
```

Thread 1: My Outreach

Step 6 – Send Invite:
"I help inspire founders and teams, am very involved in startup mentoring and really enjoy being part of human successes. Would love to connect with you as I further keep track of the evolving dynamic investor/startup world. Thank you for connecting."

Step 8 – Thank You:
"Thank you for connecting and including me in your network, truly appreciated."

Step 9's Message:
"FRAK published a pretty informative fractional report for 2024 that is worth reading. Some interesting data:

- *100k+ fractionals*
- *59% are between 44 and 59 years old*
- *12% earn over $250k a year, 30% earn <$50k per year*
- *83% of people go fractional because of flexibility*

And a whole bunch more.

State of Fractional Industry Report, Summer 2024 – read it here: https://frak.ck.page/02b4cb388e"

Step 11's Message:
"Thanks for being part of my network. Found this article about VC firms and the growing pressure on liquidity – not sure of its applicability or if you have insights on supportive or contradictory views?

https://www.wsj.com/articles/vc-firms-and-tech-startups-face-growing-pressure-for-liquidity-enter-private-equity-043f72f9

Step 13's Message:
"I'm working with a few startups as part of mentoring and coaching through TiE Atlanta. Recently, my key takeaway was how critical it is for the founders to have instilled a solid servicing culture in a way that the core group, inner circle, and balance of the team are aligned – it is clear this is CRITICAL to success.

I'm curious to know at what stage you get involved with companies through the acquisition or investment cycle. And how do you evaluate the cultural scale and readiness of the team? To what extent are they aligned toward a common set of foundational principles – and how many companies say they have these principles, and don't? Would love to hear your thoughts."

Step 14's Message:
"Trusting you're well. Tracking your activities and would love to learn more. Would

you be open to a meet and greet call or meetup?"

Thread 2: Software Developer

Step 6 – Send Invite:
"As a peer developer figuring out how to embrace and realize AI solutions, I would love to connect with you as I further keep track of this dynamic evolving space. Thank you for connecting."

Step 8 – Thank You:
"Thank you for connecting and including me in your network, truly appreciated."

Step 9's Message:
"This 'Emergent Coding' thing seems to be taking off. The decentralized development paradigm is properly challenging current development frameworks. The upfront work is not insignificant; however, the downstream benefits are astronomical. We are seeing component adoption and an interesting dynamic in specialization and collaboration. The reverse integration and marketplace model are causing us to re-tool a good number of skills – I am in the middle of helping our dev team specialize in niche areas. Would love to bend your ear on what you are seeing ahead of us."

Step 11's Message

"Thanks for being part of my network.

"Have you seen the Verge article on what's happening with AI talent right now? All out to recruit top AI researchers. There are only some 1,000 people capable of developing the latest models.

https://www.theverge.com/2024/12/20/24326135/ai-talent-wars-databricks-interview

The money going into AI is ridiculous, OpenAI's 18-month Orion project's costs are already hitting half a billion dollars!

https://www.wsj.com/tech/ai/openai-gpt5-orion-delays-639e7693

Curious to know what you are seeing!"

Step 13's Message:

"Combining systematic innovation methods with agile practices seems to offer a structured flexible development approach. What are your thoughts on the introduction of problem-solving and efficient project management to adapt swiftly to market changes and user feedback? I am curious if you have any insights or views on TRIZ or design thinking – specifically for startups."

Step 14's Message:
"Trusting this finds you well. Tracking your activities and would love to learn more. Would you be open to a meet and greet call or meetup?"

Thread 3: Small Business

Step 6 – Send Invite:
"As a peer small business owner, I would love to connect with you as I further keep track of the evolving dynamic introduction of AI, bio-composites, and analog HD. Thank you for connecting."

Step 8 – Thank You:
"Thank you for connecting and including me in your network, truly appreciated."

Step 9's Message:
"Advancements in digital recording technology have significantly improved the sound quality of vinyl records. This is part of what is making a difference for us.

By recording music digitally and then transferring it to vinyl, artists can achieve clarity and detail previously unattainable, blending analog warmth with digital precision. This is further amplified through HD for Vinyl.

We are currently investigating digital audio workstation tools including Pro Tools, Logic Pro, and Cubase. Do you have any exposure to these utilities?"

Step 11's Message:
"Thanks for being part of my network.

You'll love this. The Tennessean *talked about this new place in Nashville called The Vinyl Lab. It's a live music venue that also presses records! What a creative blend of music and manufacturing. Inspiring does not begin to describe this – watch this space.*

https://www.tennessean.com/story/entertainment/music/2024/12/18/nashville-vinyl-lab-records-dolly-parton-guns-n-roses/74972199007/."

Step 13's Message:
"We have been on a journey of environmentally eco-friendly materials and processes. We have had some exposure to the Australian band Lime Cordiale who collaborated with Brisbane's Suitcase Records and the release of an album using a bio-vinyl process reducing carbon emissions by 92%. Do you have any insights or references on this trend and technology?"

Step 14's Message:
"I trust that you are doing well. I've been tracking your activities and would love to learn

more. Would you be open to a meet and greet call or meetup?"

Thread 4: Machinist

Step 6 – Send Invite:
"As a fellow machinist, I would love to connect with you as I further keep track of the evolving dynamic space of AI entering the CNC world. Thank you for connecting."

Step 8 – Thank You:
"Thank you for connecting and including me in your network, truly appreciated."

Step 9's Message:
"Pressing AI into smart factories underpinned with industry 4.0 principles is changing my world fast. This IOT thing is happening faster than I expected. High-Speed Machining helps to optimize tool paths and cut speeds, reducing cycle times. This is all very exciting. The unplanned consequences are raw material sourcing and misaligned component delivery for final assembly.

Are you tracking this evolution? It seems to be changing faster than I can keep up with."

Step 11's Message
"Thanks for being part of my network.

*"Further to my last note, **AI and Machine Learning** integration into CNC machining allows for real-time monitoring and optimization of my processes. This has enabled predictive maintenance, adaptive control, and improved decision-making, reducing downtime and injuries.*

Our improvement ratios seem slightly ahead of market predictions. Wanted to pass on where I have kicked a toe or two and figured out some neat techniques. Let me know if you have a few minutes to chat."

Step 13 Send Message

"Seems automation and robotics are game-changers for CNC machining. It's like the future of manufacturing is already here. Check this out:

https://www.fictiv.com/articles/the-future-of-cnc-machining-2024-and-beyond?

Some interesting trends from BlueBay – demand in aerospace and defense is booming. Feels like we are getting back to the cutting edge!

https://www.bluebayautomation.com/blog/welding-metals-13/cnc-machining-trends-to-watch-in-2024-69

What's your take on this?"

Step 14's Message:
"I hope you are doing well. I've been tracking your activities and would love to learn more. Would you be open to a meet and greet call or meetup?"

Example 4: Targeted Message to the 1st Degree

This is a particular campaign sent to a specific set of people. It's typically short-lived with the aim of doing something intentional. One of the messages below went to 25 people, of which 11 offered one-on-one meetings and deep dives.

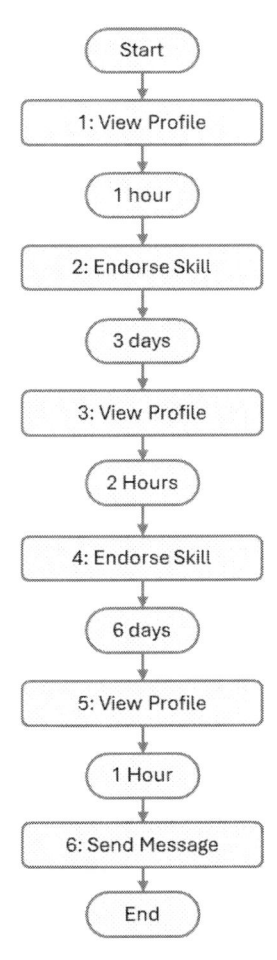

```
Start
  ↓
1: View Profile
  ↓
1 hour
  ↓
2: Endorse Skill
  ↓
3 days
  ↓
3: View Profile
  ↓
2 Hours
  ↓
4: Endorse Skill
  ↓
6 days
  ↓
5: View Profile
  ↓
1 Hour
  ↓
6: Send Message
  ↓
End
```

Step 6's Message – To VCs asking for coaching:
"Thanks for being part of my network.

I'd like to pick your brain if I may.

One of my most significant values is my ability to dramatically inspire founders. I help validate that their baby is going in the right direction and makes sense, maximizing time while using money effectively. My heartfelt and compassionate approach, linked to the importance of accountability and intensity, and sound business understanding are phenomenal assets.

It is clear to me my best business partners are either the founders themselves or the VC/PE companies backing and supporting them.

My ask is for some of your time so that I can learn how investment companies engage with founders to help them and/or hold them accountable, and at what stage the investment company, based on category, are able to help press or enable the founders.

I'd like to get guidance from you about the investor world and my value proposition in it. I am not looking to sell anything or time, I would just love to pick your brain if you are open to it – simply to maximize myself moving forward.

Much appreciated – and thank you for the nudges – I truly appreciate you."

Step 6's Message – to CEOs and Founders:
"Thanks for being part of my network.

I'd like to pick your brain if I may.

I am spending a lot of time supporting founders and CEOs of small companies in dealing with current operational efficiencies, norms, etc. I appear to be phenomenally good at affecting their lives.

I'd like to ask if I may have some time with you to gain from your learnings, should your mad schedule allow for it. I'm interested in finding out more about your operational and technical approach, funding, GTM, forecasting, resourcing, tools, etc. I'd use these learnings to pass on to other founders.

I am an active part of TiE Atlanta and YearUp, and support startups coming through TechStars, Atlanta Tech Village, and Alpharetta Tech – all voluntarily. I support a lot of entrepreneurs from around the world through mentoring platforms like ADPList and PushFar.

I'd like to get guidance from you about the investor world and my value proposition in it. I am not looking to sell anything or time, I would just love to pick your brain if you are open to it – simply to maximize myself moving forward.

Much appreciated – and thank you for the nudges – I truly appreciate you."

Step 6's Message – to Engaged Connections:

"Terribly excited. I will have the first prints of Leading Magnanimously *at the end of February 2025, and the ability to send the e-book at the end of March. The book's launch date is August 12th.*

Would love to get you a copy of the book. If you want the e-book, please send me your email address.

For printed books, I will carry the cost of the book and ask you to carry shipping charges. If you are interested, please let me know and I will follow up with the shipping URL closer to the time.

Andrew

P.S. Thanks again for your support and interest. This is equally exciting and nerve-racking!"

They Want to Meet!

Firstly, timely responses are vital. Next, make sure your responses are relevant, informative, engaging, and memorable. Your goal is to create engagement.

Part of your response toolkit must be an extremely simple way for the new contact to book time with you. I recommend you leverage a calendaring tool similar to those referenced earlier. This allows them to see your availability, compare it to their schedule, and book time in your calendar.

You need to make this step as easy as possible and avoid the to-and-fro trying to find a matching time slot and the resultant drop-off.

My calendar includes options for Executive Networking, Business Networking, and Face-to-Face Networking. This allows me to segment people based on the opportunities they offer: Someone trying to sell something is different from someone networking or a business opportunity. Many people prefer the face-to-face option.

Executives will make 20 minutes available in a heartbeat. If you are not dealing with executives, make the slots longer as you experience your ICPs. My networking sessions are booked for 20 minutes, which allows for a polite runover of 10 minutes where there is mutual value. I recommend your initial sessions be no longer than 30 minutes.

Where do you meet? Having as many options as possible available is crucial. Remember – it is your job to meet that person where they prefer. Do they want to meet via Zoom? Do a Zoom session. Google Meet or Teams? So be it. A phone call? Sure thing. If they want to meet face-to-face – then that's where you are going.

Your meeting title is critical. Make it clear and simple. Include the contact's name, your name, and the intent of the meeting. Examples would include:

- John Smith / Andrew Brummer Executive Networking
- John Smith / Andrew Brummer Tech Brainstorm
- John Smith / Andrew Brummer AI Deep Dive

- John Smith / Andrew Brummer Book Talk
- Face-to-Face | John Smith / Andrew Brummer Networking

The body of your invite should include all of the pertinent information about the event, the questions you asked when they booked time with you, and information about you. Make it easy for the person you are meeting with to find information about you and why this session is happening.

When Someone Asks to Meet

I have a standard response when someone asks to meet with me. This results in a near 90%+ booking ratio.

> "I would absolutely love to meet with you. My schedule is a bit of a mess right now with all the volunteer work I am doing. Please take a look at my schedule and let me know what slot best matches your availability.
>
> https://calendly.com/ardunan
>
> Andrew"

They get this:

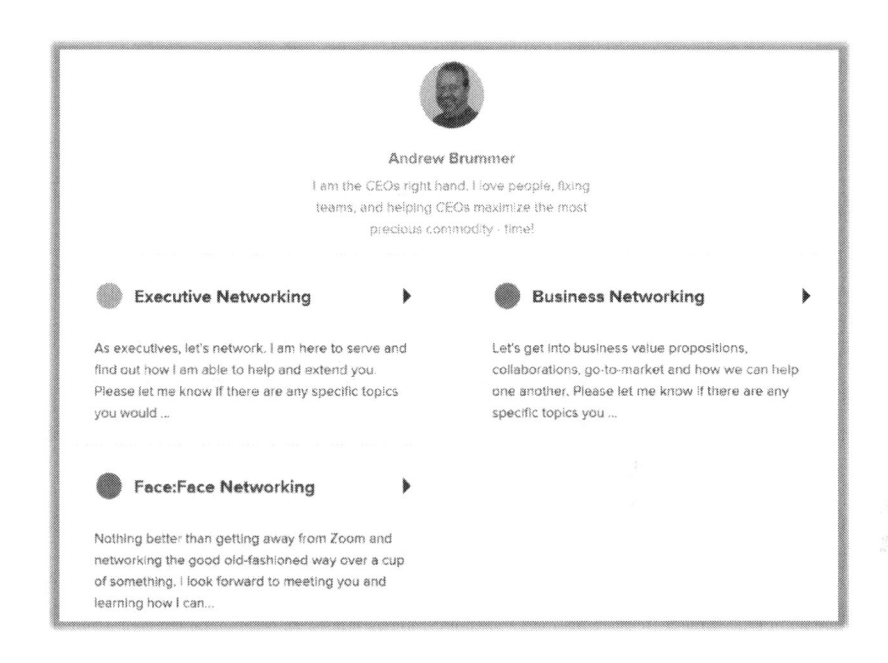

> **Andrew Brummer**
>
> I am the CEOs right hand. I love people, fixing teams, and helping CEOs maximize the most precious commodity - time!
>
> ● **Executive Networking** ▶
>
> As executives, let's network. I am here to serve and find out how I am able to help and extend you. Please let me know if there are any specific topics you would ...
>
> ● **Business Networking** ▶
>
> Let's get into business value propositions, collaborations, go-to-market and how we can help one another. Please let me know if there are any specific topics you ...
>
> ● **Face:Face Networking** ▶
>
> Nothing better than getting away from Zoom and networking the good old-fashioned way over a cup of something. I look forward to meeting you and learning how I can...

Executive Networking Option

Landing Page Summary

"As executives, let's network. I am here to serve and find out how I am able to help and extend you.

Please let me know if there are any specific topics you would like to cover."

Event Body

Event Name: [Insert the event name]
Event Description: [Insert the landing page test]
Meeting Location

Questions and Answers: [That you posed up front]

Purpose:

The purpose of this session is to network with you and to learn some insights about you and how I may serve you.

About me:

My product is people. My superpower is helping the CEO use time and money efficiently while helping generate income. My magic is helping build culturally relevant and strong teams around the CEO to prevent the "lonely at the top" syndrome.

Currently, I am networking and building a solid foundation and I look forward to meeting you and finding out how I can serve you.

You can find my LinkedIn profile here."

Business Networking Option

Landing Page Summary

"Let's get into business value propositions, collaborations, go-to-market and how we can help one another.

Please let me know if there are any specific topics you would like to cover."

Event Body

[Similar to Event Body above]

Tech Brainstorming Session

Landing Page Summary

"Let's deep dive into the latest tech evolutions. I am here to serve and find out how I am able to help and extend you.

Please let me know if there are any specific topics you would like to cover."

Event Body

[Similar to Event Body above]

AI Deep Dive Session

Landing Page Summary

"OpenAI, Grok, Gemini, and CoPilot are plowing millions into the development of the tech — let's dig. I am here to serve and find out how I am able to help and extend you.

Please let me know if there are any specific topics you would like to cover."

Event Body

[Similar to Event Body above]

Book Talk Session

Landing Page Summary

"Fantastic reading list and leadership evolution, let's run through the latest additions. I am here to serve and find out how I am able to help and extend you.

Please let me know if there are any specific topics you would like to cover."

Event Body
[Similar to Event Body above]

Face-to-face Networking

Landing Page Summary
"Nothing better than getting away from Zoom and networking the good old-fashioned way over a cup of something.

I look forward to meeting you and learning how I can serve. Please let me know if there are any specific topics you would like to cover."

Event Body
"For the day - My phone number is 404 915 2027

The purpose of this session is to network with you over a cup of coffee in the Alpharetta area and to learn how I may serve you."

Be Memorable!

You have one chance to imprint who you are in this stranger's mind – one chance. Go back and re-read the "Make Yourself Memorable" section on page 51.

Engaging with your new contact
Now that you have the meeting booked, you need to engage with the person. Be ready for them, be insightful, have questions, be memorable, and pay interest. You need them to walk away and remember you.

Speak value – not job title
Keep in mind they probably know 100 people who kind of do what you do; you need to stand out. I recommend you stay away from your job title and focus on getting to know them. Be human with them. People do business with people they know and like. Telling them what you are capable of doing does not serve you at all, nor does it make you memorable. Most frustratingly: it won't make you relevant. Being human will.

Show up with intent
Show an interest in them. Engage with them like they are your first meeting for the day. You need to be completely present, completely ready, and energetic. You should be ready with engaging questions and turn the interrogation into a discussion.

Every discussion is a brand-new discussion, every time

Make sure your open time slots and networking are in slots of the day where you have an abundance of energy. Keep your normal workday blocked in slots so that you don't worry about work during these meetings. Have that extra cup of coffee. Keep a stash of chocolates, energy drinks, or whatever gets you perky. Get up and do some jumping jacks before the meeting, or run up and down the staircase once or twice. When its' time for the meeting, ARRIVE.

Have your stories ready

I do everything to draw the discussion away from the traditional "Hi, my name is Andrew, I do A, B, C for X, Y, Z." Instead, I speak about the background they'll see in digital meetings which includes the minions, flags, VIP concert tickets, artwork done for me, collector bottles, mugs, startup memorabilia, movie props... ANYTHING to break the expected cycle.

Topics I introduce include the Christmas lights I put up over the festive season, the people I meet, the songs that play, the live-edge woodwork I do, my volunteer work, mentoring, and the love for this country.

No, I do not run through everything. I drive into the discussion on a topic or two relevant to the person I am meeting. Similarly, I engage in reciprocal discussion and questions as the discussion unfolds so that I get to know who I have the privilege of meeting.

Get to know the person
Pay attention and show interest in the person you are meeting. Their words, how they dress, what they say about their kids, pets, background, how they feel about sports, art, flowers, what their voice inflections sound like, how they animate their gestures. Ask about their hobbies and how they fill their spare time.

Be vulnerable and humble
Your goal is to get this to a discussion as quickly as you can. Get away from the masks and formalities. Be as vulnerable as is relevant and comfortable. I have experienced some earth-shattering discussion topics with absolute strangers within the small 30-minute window that has bonded us for life. Other people have gone, and we won't miss one another.

Why?
The reason I do this is to find people I could do business with; when I know the person, it is far easier to match the work and their work/life ethic than it is to match someone who can deliver on scope.

If people choose not to engage the way I do, or present themselves as stand-offish and uninterested, I am happy to let them go their way. They will find a more constructive use of their energy than battling with me. The same is true for me.

A Comprehensive Strategy

Tracking Your Relationship

It is cardinal that you have a CRM to track the discussion content, the sense you got of the person, whether you would work with them, and what kind of follow-up is needed (and how often).

Managing relationships can easily become a mess downstream if you are not deliberate here. This will allow you to track the person's career progress, information you have passed on, and information, introductions, and references they have done for you.

Your automation will stop when they contact you. Do not engage in automated contact for that connection again. You need to get into a cycle of manual contact where you are, at the right time, reason, and content, to engage with that person.

This is the most challenging part of the whole journey – making sure you remain in contact and remain relevant. DO NOT let them become another version of your LinkedIn contacts that you lost touch with. While it is time-consuming, maintaining these contacts will be far easier than 1) starting again, and 2) getting caught in a desperate situation where you need help.

Disengaged Contacts

You will absolutely experience contacts that disengage, remove you as a connection, and/or ignore you. Let them go. A well-rounded, healthy brand management campaign will serve you well over the coming months. The time and energy you yield into trying to keep people linked to you is not worth it.

An Adoption Roadmap

- LinkedIn Premium
- LinkedIn Premium ($100 per year)
- Existing Contacts (free)
- Figure out your ICP (time)
- Connect manually (time)
- Automation tool - A/B testing (~$50 per month)
- CRM tool ($30 per month)
- Calendaring tool (~$30 per month)
- Sales Navigator ($100 per month)

Networking – Supercharged

- Get your campaign going
- Volunteer
- Meetup with people
- Get Blogging
- Write a book
- Join networking Events
- Attend conferences
- Start coaching
- Attend Video presentations
- Connect people
- Professional groups
- Food Kitchens

Go do you!

What does your journey look like now? What are you going to do? What are your goals? How do you plan to take ownership and supercharge your networking? What does your network look like in four months? Who will you meet? What events will you be part of? What friends will you make? What will you uncover that you would never have been exposed to? How will you break your status quo?

I would love to hear from you and elaborate on this story; even make your experiences part of a shared journey. Please send any learnings and observations to me so that we can help one another grow and expand. We all face this impending horizon underpinned by AI and complicated by the changing world of hybrid, remote, and in-person employment – as society grapples with re-establishing how we foster relationships and develop one another.

Read, read, read. Feed your mind. Grow your soul.

Thank you for taking this journey with me. I cannot wait to hear from you at Editor@YouDecideTomorrow.com.

Curious? Wanna talk?

If you have got through this all, and have questions, want to know more, want to hear from others, join us at Li.youdecide.us or Li.ardunan.com for collaborative share and ask me anything. If this link does not take you to a LinkedIn event page, please email andrew@youdecide.us

Relevant Reads

- *Trusted Advisor* – David H. Maister
- *Good to Great* – Jim Collins
- *Radical Candor* – Kim Scott
- *Crucial Conversations* – Kerry Patterson
- *No Excuses!* – Brian Tracy
- *Influencer* – Kerry Patterson, Joseph Grenny, & David Maxfield
- *Atomic Habits* – James Clear
- *Pitch Anything* – Oren Klaff
- *Designing Your Life* – Bill Burnett
- *Digital Body Language* – Erica Dhawan
- *Lean In* – Sheryl Sandberg
- *Mindset* – Carol Dweck
- *Think Again* – Adam Grant
- *The Digital Mindset* – Paul Leonardi
- *Daring Greatly* – Brené Brown
- *10x Is Easier Than 2x* – Dan Sullivan & Benjamin Hardy
- *How to Win Friends and Influence People* – Dale Carnegie
- *Multipliers*, Revised – Liz Wiseman, Stephen Covey—foreword
- *Blue Ocean Strategy* – W. Chan Kim & Renee Mauborgne

- *Change Anything* – Kerry Patterson, Joseph Grenny, David Maxfield, Ron McMillan, & Al Switzler
- *Start with Why* – Simon Sinek
- *Kind transparency* – Amanda Frye

Made in the USA
Columbia, SC
28 January 2025